you know you're in
illinois when...

Some Other Books in the Series

You Know You're in Arizona When . . .

You Know You're in Florida When . . .

You Know You're in Kansas When . . .

You Know You're in Michigan When . . .

You Know You're in Minnesota When . . .

You Know You're in New Hampshire When . . .

You Know You're In Series

you know you're in
illinois when...

101 quintessential places, people, events, customs, lingo, and eats of the prairie state

Pam Henderson and Jan Mathew

INSIDERS' GUIDE®

GUILFORD, CONNECTICUT
AN IMPRINT OF THE GLOBE PEQUOT PRESS

INSIDERS' GUIDE ®

Copyright © 2006 by Morris Book Publishing, LLC

Text design by Linda R. Loiewski
Illustrations by Sue Mattero

Library of Congress Cataloging-in-Publication Data
Henderson, Pam.
    You know you're in Illinois when—:101 quintessential places, people, events, customs, lingo, and eats of the Prairie State / Pam Henderson and Jan Mathew. —1st ed.
        p. cm. — (You know you're in series)
    Includes index.
    ISBN 0-7627-3917-7
    1. Illinois—Miscellanea. 2. Illinois—Guidebooks. 3. Illinois—Humor. 4. Illinois—Description and travel—Miscellanea. I. Mathew, Jan, 1958– II.Title. III. Series.

    F541.6.H47 2006
    977.3'043—dc22

                                                          2005025933

Manufactured in the United States of America
First Edition/First Printing

To Granny Cole for handing down her love of words. (PH)

To the beloved "core" who shared my earliest Illinois adventures — Ruth, Roger, Joy, and Joni. (JM)

about the authors

Pam Henderson was reared on a diversified livestock and grain farm in central Illinois that continues to support four farming generations. A graduate of the University of Illinois, this award-winning writer has worked for *Prairie Farmer* as well as *Farm Journal.* Beyond agriculture, she writes frequently about the state of Illinois for newspapers and magazines.

A native of the central Illinois flatlands and graduate of the University of Illinois at Urbana-Champaign, writer **Jan Mathew** often yearned to live someplace far more exotic than the Land of Lincoln. She managed to get as far as neighboring Iowa and Indiana before leapfrogging back to her home state in 2000—and deciding that "exotic" lies in the eye of the beholder.

to the reader

Illinois defies definition. To many it simply means Chicago. To those of us born on the prairie, it is the black loam that yields pearly soybeans and golden corn. To some it is swimming in Lake Michigan, and to others it is watching the powerful Mississippi merge with the Ohio in Illinois' southland.

Illinois is skyscrapers, barns, flatlands, craggy peaks, John Belushi, and Carl Sandburg. Sophisticated. Rural. Cultured. Country. Not even baseball can draw a consensus. If you doubt this, just go watch the Chicago Cubs battle the St. Louis Cardinals.

Selecting and researching entries for this book treated us to scavenger hunts and history lessons. The first Illinoisans left massive mounds to mark their passing. The seeds of three presidents took root in the prairie soil. Illinois is the home of Horseshoe sandwiches, Snickers bars, deep-dish pizzas, and dressed-up hot dogs and is stuck together with Wrigley chewing gum. We protect snakes and white squirrels, pay homage to industrialists like John Deere, speak our own language, cringe at political corruption, and keep our sense of humor intact by erecting monuments to Superman and Popeye.

Almost 400 miles long from top to toe, Illinois is hemmed by water and is influenced by five neighboring states. Not even the temperature is consistent, varying by nearly 10 degrees from north to south on any given day. Here Hemingway lived, Frank Lloyd Wright built, and Lincoln walked.

It is a fascinating place, but mostly it is home.

illinois
... four-leaf clovers form a club

4-H kids are as American as apple pie. Better yet, most of them can actually bake an apple pie. 4-H is a youth group aimed at teaching practical life skills and building better citizens. It started in 1899 in Illinois and spread to all 50 states and to 80 countries. Today 4-H is the world's largest educational program outside the classroom; seven million American kids participate in it, nearly 300,000 of them from Illinois.

These days, members are just as likely to be urban kids learning about computers and communications as cows and cooking. But the farm-fresh 4-H image comes from the organization's rural roots. At the turn of the century, W. B. Otwell, secretary of the Macoupin County Illinois Farmer's Institute, planted the first seeds of 4-H when he gave small packages of seed corn to 500 boys. They were encouraged to grow the corn and exhibit it for prizes. Corn-growing, pig-raising, and food-preservation clubs began to emerge, and in 1914 Congress authorized funds to support boys' and girls' club work. Land-grant universities joined with parent and local volunteers to complete the 4-H community.

Blue ribbons are still part of the experience. Club members exhibit their projects before county fair judges each summer, and those who excel advance to state fair competitions. No matter the outcome, the 4-H

4-H:

Youth organization started in Illinois that helps teach children around the world practical skills and how to be better citizens.

motto is "to make the best better." Standing before the symbolic green four-leaf clover, 4-H kids from ages 5 to 19 pledge "my head to clearer thinking; my heart to greater loyalty; my hands to larger service; and my health to better living for my club, my community, my country, and my world." That's as wholesome as a glass of milk with that apple pie.

For more information on Illinois 4-H, visit www.4-h.uiuc.edu.

illinois
... actors come out to play

Mork wasn't really from Ork—he was born in Chicago. So was the Corellian pilot Han Solo. Dick Grayson, aka Robin, was a Gotham City transplant from Winnetka.

Illinois actors are no strangers to the screen or stage. Robin Williams, Harrison Ford, and Chris O'Donnell join Charlton Heston, Rock Hudson, Sam Shepard, and Raquel Welch on the state's family tree. So do funny men Jack Benny, John Belushi, Bill Murray, Bob Newhart, and Richard Pryor.

Who needs Hollywood? Among the memorable films made in Illinois are *The Sting; The Blues Brothers; Sixteen Candles; The Breakfast Club; Ferris Bueller's Day Off; The Color of Money; About Last Night; The Untouchables; Planes, Trains, and Automobiles; When Harry Met Sally; The Fugitive;* and the *Home Alone* series. Woodstock and Crystal Lake doubled as Punxsutawney, Pennsylvania, in *Groundhog Day.* The Urbana-Champaign campus of the University of Illinois became Harvard University in *With Honors.* Given this list, it seems fitting that movie criticism came to the masses from Chicago's own dueling film reviewers Roger Ebert and Gene Siskel.

As for Broadway, there is no need to travel 800 miles to New York when the best shows will come to you in Chicago. From the revitalized North Loop Theatrical District to neighboring communities, stage lovers can select from classical Shake-speare to improvisational comedy. Historic venues like the Cadillac Palace Theatre, a restored vaudevillian showcase, and the Ford Center for the Performing Arts, with its gilded ceilings and Far Eastern decor, are taking well-deserved encores. At the Step-penwolf Theatre Company, being backstage is often like attending a homecoming. Illinoisans Gary Sinise and John Malkovich are among the theater's best known members.

Downstate, all types of theater flourish. In Bloomington the oldest continuously performed passion play in the United States is staged with spiritual fervor, and the Shake-speare Festival has filled the Elizabethan-style theater on the grounds of Ewing Manor since 1978.

Actors:

A source of pride in Illinois, where homegrown thespians bring talent to the stage and screen.

illinois
...the nuclear age dawns

Atoms and buffalo seem strange bedfellows. But just outside Chicago in Batavia, a herd of American bison call the nation's most important physics laboratory home.

Fermilab is also home to the Tevatron, the world's highest-energy particle accelerator and collider. Here counter-rotating beams of protons and antiprotons smash together, allowing scientists to examine the basic building blocks of matter and the forces acting on them. The mission is to unlock nature's deepest secrets and to learn how the universe is made and how it works.

Despite urban legends to the contrary, the buffalo roaming the grounds are not living Geiger counters or the equivalent of a canary in a mineshaft. Traditional symbols of the raw frontier prairie, these animals represent the lab's involvement in the frontier of high-energy physics. They are not the only ones who enjoy the scenery: Fermilab encourages visitors to explore the 6,800-acre campus by hiking on the restored prairie and bicycling a series of trails.

Unlikely as it sounds, the first atomic reaction was generated on a squash court located beneath the west stands of the University of Chicago's football stadium. On December 2, 1941, Nobel Prize–winning physicist Enrico Fermi achieved the first self-sustaining chain reaction that led to the creation of nuclear energy. It was all part of the Manhattan Project and a hush-hush

Atoms:

Building blocks for nuclear energy researched in two Illinois laboratories.

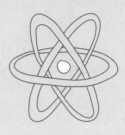

frenzy to beat Hitler's Nazi machine in the production of atomic weapons.

It doesn't take a quantum leap to see that Illinois is an energetic place. Argonne National Laboratory, one of the U.S. Department of Energy's largest research centers, carries out its work on 1,500 wooded acres in DuPage County (about 25 miles southwest of Chicago). Scientists at Argonne deliver energy, environmental, and national security solutions. They are involved in creating hybrid cars and alternative fuels and in studying proteins that can accurately target disease. The lab also offers cool science classes for students and teachers.

For more information on Illinois' famous labs, visit www.fnal.gov and www.anl.gov.

illinois

...great writers get a little wordy

Long heralded as fertile ground for corn and beans, Illinois also cultivates literary creativity—bushels of best sellers, penned by native sons and daughters. Famed writers who found their muse in the Prairie State include Carl Sandburg, Vachel Lindsay, and Ernest Hemingway.

Sandburg, born on January 6, 1878, recounted his boyhood in the small town of Galesburg in his autobiography, *Always the Young Strangers*. Intrigued by history and inspired by the common man, he wrote prolifically about Abraham Lincoln and the Civil War in a tome that won the 1940 Pulitzer Prize for history. Sandburg also tucked polished nuggets from his Illinois past into folk songs and poetry. Visitors to his three-room cottage birthplace can read Sandburg's celebrated prose etched on stepping stones leading to Remembrance Rock, where his ashes are buried.

"Prairie Troubadour" Lindsay wandered the Midwest on foot, reciting his poetry in exchange for food and shelter. But the Illinois capital of Springfield, where he was born on November 10, 1879, anchored the eccentric performance poet. Though he often chronicled life's lighter side, Lindsay crafted a dark conclusion to his own story, committing suicide in 1931. Today the home where he was born and died is authentically restored and houses many of Lindsay's works of art and writings.

Authors:

Famous writers with literary roots in Illinois, including Carl Sandburg, Vachel Lindsay, and Ernest Hemingway.

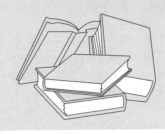

Hemingway's Pulitzer Prize–winning novels transported readers to places as distant as Mount Kilimanjaro and the streets of Spain, but his journey began in a second-floor bedroom in his Oak Park home, where he was delivered by his father, Dr. Clarence Hemingway, on July 21, 1899. The western Chicago suburb also witnessed Hemingway's first published works: stories for the Oak Park High School literary magazine, *Trapeze*. Almost as thrilling as Spanish bullfights are Hemingway's childhood diary and photos, displayed in his birthplace and in the nearby Hemingway Museum.

Such literary masters may have inspired other creative thinkers from Illinois, including L. Frank Baum, Edgar Lee Burroughs, Upton Sinclair, Gwendolyn Brooks, Saul Bellow, Michael Crichton, and Scott Turow.

4

illinois

... the stars are crossed

Bald Knob Mountain in the southern Illinois Ozarks has a higher calling than most. On this country peak, a white cross called the Bald Knob Cross of Peace rises more than 700 feet above the valley below. Illuminated at night, the symbol shines like a beacon of hope for 7,500 square miles.

The peaceful sight inspires thousands to take a closer look each year. A country road outside the tiny village of Alto Pass winds past peach orchards and wildflower-filled forests to deliver visitors to the foot of the cross.

The marble base sits 1,034 feet above sea level, and the reinforced porcelain steel structure reaches 111 feet into the heavens. With arms stretching a total of 63 feet wide, Bald Knob Cross welcomes all who seek comfort. The grassy clearing surrounding the cross is in constant use for retreats and weddings. Motorcyclists from across the United States gather here during the last weekend in April for the annual Blessing of the Bikes.

The story of how the cross evolved lies somewhere between happenstance and divine inspiration. A simple conversation between a local pastor and a rural mail carrier resulted in a plan to hold an Easter sunrise service on the mountaintop in 1937. Worshippers were awed by the dawn lighting the distant hills, and the event became a tradition. By the early 1950s the Easter service was such a draw that a new dream began to take shape.

Local residents saved their pennies and joined forces to build a permanent shrine. They wanted the cross to stand as a national symbol of faith, to help bolster the spiritual fiber of America. In true rural Illinois fashion, one woman gave as her tithe a litter of pigs. Her simple gesture multiplied into a hog-rearing project that eventually raised enough money to finish the project without breaking the bank.

Bald Knob Cross:

A giant cross, located in southern Illinois, that serves as a symbol of peace.

illinois
... you find a peanut gallery

Going nuts in Illinois is no problem. Head to Bloomington and the Beer Nuts company store to load up on the flavored snack nut.

Of course, all you really have to do to find Beer Nuts is walk into a bar or grocery anywhere in America. Over the past 60 years, the glazed peanut and the red-and-white, oval Beer Nuts logo have become as popular as peanut butter.

The official company history started in 1937, when Edward Shirk and his son Arlo took over the Caramel Crisp confectionery store. The ancestors of today's Beer Nuts were known as "redskins" because they were prepared with their red skins intact. These peanuts were occasionally offered at no charge to entice patrons to buy more soda pop. In the early 1950s the family started selling the product as Shirk's Glazed Peanuts in local liquor stores.

Then, in 1953, a potato chip distributor named Eldridge Brewster talked the family into packaging the nuts on a larger scale. Selling the tasty treats to taverns by promoting them as a way to sell more beer turned out to be a great idea. Pulling out a package of Beer Nuts has become the equivalent of saying, "Let's get the party started!" Just remember the company's motto: "Please snack responsibly."

Contrary to popular belief, there is no beer in Beer Nuts. The ingredients are simple enough: peanuts, oil, corn syrup, and salt. But the coating process is a big secret. While the product line now includes other nuts, peanuts are still the top seller.

Members of the Shirk family still run the business today, using the same unique formula in the same town where the nutty phenomenon of combining the slight tang of peanuts in the skin with a sweet-salty glaze began. The production plant is not open to the public, but you can buy the nuts and logo merchandise in the company's Outlet Shoppe. The infamous empty Beer Nuts can stuffed with a springy artificial snake is legendary as a practical prank. For more information, visit www.beernuts.com.

Beer Nuts:

A brand of snack foods featuring peanuts coated with a sweet-and-salty glaze.

illinois
... pets butt into baseball

In retrospect, Chicago Cubs fans would agree: October 6, 1945, should have been "Bring Your Goat to a Baseball Game" day at Wrigley Field. On that fateful afternoon, the Cubs—National League champs for the first time in 37 years—took to the field against the Detroit Tigers, needing only two more wins to clinch the World Series.

Among the diehards in attendance were Greek immigrant and restaurant owner William "Billy Goat" Sianis and the ace he believed could deliver the victory: his good-luck charm and pet goat, Murphy. With two $7.20 tickets in hand, Sianis coaxed the mammal toward the bleachers, only to be followed by sour-faced ushers. Seems the goat, and his offensive odor, had to go.

Sianis and Murphy went, but not without angry words that haunt the Cubs' faithful to this day: "Cubs, they not gonna win anymore," Sianis shouted.

And ever since, thanks to a curse as stubborn as the billy goat himself, the Cubbies have proven themselves America's favorite losers. They went down in Game 4 in 1945, ultimately lost that World Series, and have proceeded to suffer the longest National League championship drought in Major League Baseball history.

Those attempting to reverse the curse have struck out, too. In 1994 past Cubs manager Tom Trebelhorn arranged for a second-

Billy Goat Curse:

Angry words uttered in the 1945 World Series by William "Billy Goat" Sianis that wrought winless decades upon the Chicago Cubs.

generation Sianis and Cubs great Ernie Banks to join a group of monastic monks in a cleansing procession around Wrigley's interior vine-covered walls. No luck.

Turns out the ones loaded with good fortune are members of the Sianis family. Today the restaurant founded by William, who died in 1970, is the world-famous Billy Goat Tavern, where you're invited to "butt in anytime" for "cheezeborgers and cheeps."

Should you decide to try your hand at lifting the Billy Goat Curse, you can check out the Cubs' home schedule at www.cubs.com. Take your pick of any of six Billy Goat Tavern locations, too, all listed at www.billygoat tavern.com.

Just leave your pets at home.

illinois
...Black Hawk is a hero

Talk about a big case of mistaken identity. The 110-ton concrete statue that towers from the eastern bluffs of the Rock River, near the small town of Oregon, is known far and wide as Chief Black Hawk.

Truth is, Black Hawk was never a chief, nor was the statue built to depict his life. Native-born sculptor Lorado Taft, a major figure on Illinois' art scene in the early 20th century, created the 44-foot-tall stone-faced giant in 1911 to honor all Native Americans. It was intended to serve as a reminder of the importance of preserving the area's natural beauty. The hollow monument is made of 238 cubic yards of concrete and reinforced with two tons of twisted steel. It was poured as one piece, making it the second largest monolithic statue in the world.

The real Black Hawk was a warrior who lived in this section of Illinois in the 19th century. The recognized leader of the Sauk nation is best known for the war that bears his name. In the spring of 1831, Black Hawk and his people were forced from the Rock River region into Iowa. A year later he came back to Illinois with 1,500 followers and tried to recapture his ancestral home. The war was a 15-week disaster that ended with Black Hawk's capture and the death of more than 1,000 of his people.

Taft's huge, blanketed monument stands with arms folded, gazing out over the same

Black Hawk:

Sauk warrior whose name is affiliated with a famous statue that honors Native Americans and stands guard over the Rock River Valley.

valley from which the Sauk were sorrowfully exiled. Black Hawk lived in a time when the ancient ways were crumbling before the cultural pressure of new Americans. The tragedy and irony of his final years is that he ended up disgraced among his own people but gained fame and admiration from his former white enemies.

Black Hawk's eloquence helped make him a hero. He humbled those who settled his beloved homeland with these words: "The Rock River country was a beautiful country. I loved my towns and my cornfields, for they were home to my people. I fought for it. It is now yours. Keep it as we did."

For more information on the statue, call the Blackhawk Waterways Convention and Visitors Bureau (800–678–2108) or visit www.blackhawkwaterwayscvb.org.

illinois

... you can swing to the blues and all that jazz

Chicago has a heartbeat, a soul, a sound. Musical movements seem to transplant themselves to this fertile landscape and then cross-pollinate to emerge in distinctive styles like jazz, swing, and Chicago blues.

The city has a long tradition in jazz, putting a faster, flashier tempo into the typical New Orleans improvisational small-group style. Louis Armstrong, Jelly Roll Morton, Bix Beiderbecke, and Hoagy Carmichael are just a few who embraced this sound and made it their own. Jazz transformed into big-band swing beginning in the 1930s. King of Swing Benny Goodman grew up in the city and used his clarinet to usher in this new musical era.

But nothing typifies Chicago more than the blues. Night after night, in smoke-filled, dimly lit clubs across the city, singers croon Robert Johnson's song of heartbreak nearly to the point of weeping:

> *Come on*
> *Oh baby don't you wanna go*
> *Back to that same old place*
> *Sweet home Chicago*

The blues weren't invented in Chicago, but they were shaped here. Up from the Mississippi Delta came a lusty, soulful sound that, when played in the North, got urbanized, amplified, and set to grooves that pulse through the heart of this industrial, working-class city. Chicago blues took the country style of the South and added electric guitars, harmonicas (and an occasional drum, bass, or horn), and a big beat.

Muddy Waters, who moved to Chicago in 1943, spearheaded the new blues. It's no accident that the Rolling Stones chose their name from one of his early recordings. His song "Got My Mojo Working" still reverberates today.

So do many other classics at the Chicago Blues Festival, which celebrated its 22nd anniversary in June 2005. Each year legends share the stage with up-and-coming musicians who make sure that the city remains *the* place to get the blues.

The Blues:

Lusty, soulful music that echoes through the Windy City.

illinois
... mountains are man-made

From the Mississippi River's flat, fertile bottomlands east of St. Louis rises one of mankind's greatest mysteries. An ancient man-made mountain as tall as the Egyptian pyramids stands as evidence that a sophisticated civilization once flourished here. But where did these people go, and how could they vanish without a trace?

Historians refer to the first Illinoisans as the Mound Builders and call their city Cahokia. Found artifacts support the belief that Cahokia was once a mecca or Vatican-type sacred city that stretched some 6 square miles and grew to a population of 20,000 or more.

Of the 120 mounds that once existed, 68 are preserved today within a 2,200-acre tract of land maintained by the state as a historical site. A visitor center re-creates what life must have been like for the Cahokians, who lived here in A.D. 700 and prospered for five centuries.

The central mound dominating the site is Monk's Mound, named for a colony of Trappist monks who lived nearby in the early 1800s. It is the largest earthen construction north of Mexico, reaching 100 feet skyward and covering 14 acres. Hike up the steps carved into the side of the vast, terraced structure and imagine workers hefting baskets of soil to build it. From the platform top, a chieftain once lived and reigned. Smaller, conical mounds served as burial sites.

Hand tools found amid the rubble indicate that the members of this culture evolved beyond hunters and gatherers to become the state's first farmers. To keep track of time, and probably to set planting dates, they put poles in the ground, lining them up with the sun in a circular fashion. This system for marking solstices and equinoxes is reminiscent of England's Stonehenge, and so the ring became known as Woodhenge.

War, disease, social unrest, or a climate change affecting crop production may have led to the demise of the mounds' inhabitants. If Indians of later periods knew the tale, it was never recorded. By the time the first Europeans arrived in Illinois, the mounds were already monuments to the past. For more information, visit www.cahokiamounds.com.

Cahokia Mounds:

Earthen ceremonial and burial mounds of a prehistoric civilization, preserved as a heritage site southeast of St. Louis.

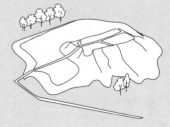

illinois

... suckers (and candy bars) are made every day

Move over Willy Wonka. Ride the "L" in downtown Chicago, and you'll find the air filled with the intoxicating aroma of chocolate. Blommer Chocolate Factory, located just north of the Loop, is the largest cocoa bean processor in the United States. They roast the beans 24/7 and supply chocolate and specialty cocoas to candy makers around the world.

It only gets sweeter in Chicago. Home to more than 100 candy companies, the city is considered the nation's candy capital. The Mars plant on Chicago's west side still produces most of the Milky Way, Snickers, and Three Musketeers bars sold in the United States. The Ferrara Pan Company uses about 200,000 pounds of sugar each day to make Jawbusters, Red Hots, Lemonheads, Atomic Fireballs, and Boston Baked Beans. And more than 60 million Tootsie Rolls, the first penny candy to be wrapped in paper, are made each day at Tootsie Roll Industries. The latter is also the world's largest lollipop manufacturer, producing 20 million pops per day.

In North Chicago another favorite rolls out by the billions each year. Jelly Belly candies rose from tasty confection to cultural icon thanks to the cravings of President Ronald Reagan, an Illinois native. Blueberry, now one of the most popular of the 150 flavors, was developed for his 1981 inauguration;

Candy Capital:

A sweet name that recognizes Chicago for its contributions to caloric intake.

three and a half tons of red, white, and blue beans were shipped to the White House for the big event.

Among other famous brands, Baby Ruth and Butterfinger got their start in Chicago with the Curtiss Candy Company (later bought out by Nestlé). Even Hershey, best known for its Pennsylvania roots, has a Chicago connection. It was at the 1893 Columbian Exposition that Milton Hershey discovered the chocolate-making equipment that would revolutionize the candy industry. The company celebrates this fact through a retail shop on Michigan Avenue, where chocolate lovers feast on fresh-baked goodies topped with Hershey products.

illinois
. . . schoolkids select the state bird

The Macomb Branch of the National Federation of Professional Women's Clubs once gave Illinois schoolchildren a somewhat bird-brained assignment: From a list of five indigenous fine-feathered friends, pick the one that best represents your state.

In flew the 7-inch cardinal, which, after cinching the 1928 popular classroom vote, became Illinois' official state bird by a bill (no pun intended) adopted in the state legislature a year later.

Perhaps color tipped the scale. Also known as redbirds, male cardinals boast a bright red coat with distinctive black markings. Brownish-gray females tone down the crimson a notch, preferring it as an accent for their wings, tail, and crest. These same bright feathers, perched atop their heads, are raised to threaten enemies.

Overall, cardinals are friendly birds that charm Illinoisans with a range of cheerful, flutelike songs. So enchanting were the tunes that, before state law stepped in, cardinals were trapped and sold as songbirds. The same edict put an end to using their brilliant feathers to decorate women's hats.

Cardinals find much to tout in their state. There's always plenty to eat—worms, beetles, codling moths, and grain in the summer, with a smorgasbord of backyard feeder food in the winter—and lots of avail-

Cardinal:

The official state bird of Illinois since 1929.

able housing sites in the form of dense shrubbery, tangled vines, saplings, and small trees. Never a materials shortage, either. The state provides weed stems, twigs, bark, and leaves in abundance.

Quality of life may explain consistent population growth. Each April through August, a female lays three or four eggs, which hatch within two weeks. Independence is encouraged, with young cardinals flying the coop within 20 days. Meanwhile, the female is busy preparing a new nest for her next brood—a cycle that sounds suspiciously like multiplication homework for today's students.

illinois
... tomatoes get the big squeeze

When it comes to condiments, 48-ounce jugs of Hunt's or Heinz have nothing on Brooks Old Original Tangy Catsup—a hot tomato mix that tops them all from a height of 170 feet in the southern Illinois community of Collinsville.

Back in 1949, when the town needed a new 100,000-gallon water tower, Gerhart S. Suppiger, president of Brooks Tomato Products Company, suggested spicing things up with a bottle-shaped structure. After all, the modest gent argued, his company made America's top-selling brand at the time, and Brooks' zesty blend not only tickled residents' taste buds, but also provided their bread and butter, so to speak.

His lark spread some serious business. The W. E. Caldwell Company was hired to construct a ramped-up replica of Brooks' distinctive, tapered catsup bottle: a 70-foot-tall riveted steel vat atop 100-foot-tall legs, capped by a 25-foot-wide lid. Dubbed the World's Largest Catsup Bottle (and who would argue?), the structure stood proudly just south of downtown along Route 159.

By 1960 bottling operations had moved to Indiana, the old factory had been converted to a warehouse, and the once-proud landmark started losing some zip. Unwilling to see their tower take its final tip, a local grassroots gang—the Catsup Bottle Preservation Group—stepped up in 1993 and raised $80,000 to repair, strip, and paint the structure.

Herculean efforts poured forth: Workers hand-painted the bottle while suspended by cables, as its irregular shape didn't accommodate scaffolding. They even penned Suppiger's original slogan: "Makes everything taste better." Residents celebrated the completion of their re-capped condiment tower on June 3, 1995, and continue to raise funds for its upkeep with occasional Catsup Bottle Celebration Days.

Visit here, and old-timers may try to sell you a tale as tall as the tower itself—that it holds enough real catsup for 26 million burger-lovers to enjoy a teaspoon each. But in case you're not buying, scout Collinsville-area stores where user-friendly sizes of Brooks Old Original Tangy Catsup are still sold.

Catsup Bottle:

At 170 feet, the world's tallest condiment-shaped water tower, located in Collinsville.

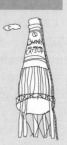

illinois

...a pirate's lair becomes a state park

Shiver me timbers! Few caves have boasted as many pirates as Cave-in-Rock, now part of a state park at the southeastern edge of Illinois. You can explore the lair for yourself and see if the scallywags left anything behind.

Cave-in-Rock, located close to the town of the same name, is more than a little famous. Disney used it when filming the 1956 children's classic *Davy Crockett and the River Pirates,* and it served as a backdrop for the 1963 epic *How the West Was Won.* But sharing credits with the likes of James Stewart, Henry Ford, and Gregory Peck is a mere footnote to the bloody past of the place.

A partially concealed entrance and a wide view of the Ohio River made Cave-in-Rock a perfect outlaw hideout. It became a stronghold for pirates who plundered flatboats and robbed and murdered travelers before the end of the Revolutionary War.

The cavern became notorious in about 1797, when Sam Mason, a renegade Virginian, began operating a tavern and gambling parlor inside. The cave was the base for the bloodthirsty Harpe brothers in the early 1800s. Counterfeiters, bandits, and an impressive assortment of other bad guys hung around here before federal troops finally rousted the rabble in 1834.

The grotto can be easily spotted along the Ohio River's north bluff; look for a graceful arched opening 55 feet wide and about 20 feet high. The cave cuts 200 feet deep into the rocky bluff, and the temperature inside hovers in the mid-50s, even on the most sultry summer day. A marked hiking trail in the 204-acre state park leads you down stone steps and along the bluff to the cave entrance.

Once inside, don't be surprised if your imagination runs riot. Some say moans of the long-departed still echo from the mouth of this old den of thieves. Cave-in-Rock State Park is located along Route 1 and offers lodging and dining. For more information, call (618) 289–4325 or (618) 289–4545.

Cave-in-Rock:

A pirate cave where bloodthirsty legends still live along the Ohio River bluffs.

illinois
...bears wear helmets

While you can't feed the Bears, you're certainly welcome to watch them at play when they growl and rumble their way across Chicago's Soldier Field.

These grizzly competitors cut their teeth on cornstarch. Originally dubbed "The Staleys," the Chicago Bears began as a company team for Staley Starch Works of Decatur, Illinois, in 1920. When a recession hit soon after and company owner A. E. Staley couldn't afford the team, he urged his young superstar, University of Illinois standout George Halas, to take the Staleys to Chicago.

The squad ran in with a hard-hitting new name—reasoning that if Chicago baseball was "Cubs," meatier-and-meaner football should be "Bears"—and Halas became "Papa Bear." A paternal owner who played defensive end, sold tickets, and coached (the latter for 40 years), he introduced the T-formation, training camp, daily practices, and curfews. Papa Bear also helped form the National Football League.

The player-to-coach evolution continued with "Iron Mike" Ditka, who drove the den from 1982 to 1992 and cinched the 1985 Super Bowl. The same year 10 Bears made pop culture history by trading cleats for dancing shoes and rapping to the "Super Bowl Shuffle," an MTV hit.

Chicago Bears:

Illinois' official National Football League team, whose home turf is Soldier Field.

Since the 1920s about 1,200 athletes have sported the team's navy and orange, selected for its resemblance to the University of Illinois' orange and blue. Legends loom large: "Galloping Ghost" Red Grange; Dick Butkus; Gale Sayers; "Sweetness" Walter Payton; William "Refrigerator" Perry; Mike Singletary; quarterback and "Shuffle" lead singer Jim McMahon; and Brian Piccolo, whose life story inspired the movie *Brian's Song*.

In 2003 Chicago gave the Bears a new place to tackle: a $580 million renovation of Soldier Field, built within the historic venue's shell. Unfortunately, archrival Green Bay showed its appreciation for the transformed turf by beating the Bears in their September 29 debut contest.

illinois
...the dogs are dressed right

Hot diggity dog. Chicago may not have invented the hot dog, but it certainly perfected it. Hot dogs, perhaps even more than deep-dish pizza, are considered the city's native food. Even a New York street vendor knows that a Chicago Dog—commonly pronounced "dawg"—demands requisite condiments and garnishes.

A Chicago-style dog comes nestled in a poppy seed bun, topped with yellow mustard, a fluorescent-green sweet pickle relish, chopped white onions, red tomato wedges, a slice or two of kosher-style dill pickle, a dash of celery salt, and a couple of hot, green sport peppers. The complete assembly is sometimes called "dragging it through the garden," but the more common term is "the works." To be frank, Chicago hot dog eaters are fine with putting anything on a dog except catsup.

A true Chicago dog is typically prepared with a locally made, skinless Vienna brand beef frank. It's steamed to a delicate crunch and never boiled, grilled, or fried. Those who wish to add to their dogs can find their plates heaped generously with piles of hand-cut fries sizzled to a reddish-brown color and soft consistency that announces they're fresh, never frozen.

There are an estimated 1,800 hot-dog stands in the Chicagoland area, more than all the local McDonald's, Wendy's, and

Chicago Dog:

A sausage sandwich dressed in all the right condiments—but no catsup.

Burger King restaurants combined. Most are run by individual entrepreneurs. In 2004 Chicagoans ate 20,552,200 hot dogs—making the city the fourth largest hot dog market in North America.

Authentic hot dog stands flourish all over the city, with cute names such as Irving's for Red Hot Lovers, Mustard's Last Stand, Poochie's, U Dawg U, Underdogg, Relish the Thought, and Superdawg. Other famous spots include Fluky's, Byron's, and Portillo's.

illinois

It lifts from the pan as a hefty wedge. Strings of melted mozzarella, tomatoes, and fresh fillings decadently ooze over flaky, thick crust. Compared to classic Italian pizza with its thin crust and delicate toppings, Chicago-style is the full meal deal.

There are an estimated 2,000-plus pizzerias in the Chicago area, and most of them offer a deep-dish option. Getting folks to agree on who cooked up this idea is almost as difficult as getting a family of four to agree on one pizza topping. History typically credits Pizzeria Uno and its founder, Ike Sewell, with starting the craze in 1943. Intent on making pizza more than a snack, Sewell found culinary inspiration for the idea in war-era one-dish casserole meals. At the time the ingredients he combined were inexpensive, readily available, and hearty. Plus the deep crust did not require the dough-handling skills of the traditional thin pies.

Although the exact recipe remains a closely held secret, Pizzeria Uno begins with a layer of mozzarella over the bottom crust, followed by tomatoes, basil, oregano, and garlic, then meat and vegetable toppings; the final touches are a liberal sprinkling of grated Parmesan cheese and a drizzle of olive oil.

The culinary masterpiece became so popular that Sewell opened a second restaurant, Pizzeria Due, just one block away. Both locations still welcome diners to the same 1940s vintage-walnut veneers and black-and-white tile floors that smack of a Chicago-style speakeasy from the Prohibition era. The only difference is that Pizzeria Uno is now franchised and spreading Illinois indulgence across the nation, one slice at a time.

Chicago-Style Pizza:

Deep-dish decadence that has become a tradition across the nation.

illinois

... baseball players once threw everything but the ball

From the south side of Chicago come the baddest boys in baseball, tough major leaguers with a sullied history and gloves of grit.

The White Sox formed in 1901 as one of the American League's eight charter teams. By 1910 owner Charles Comiskey settled the Sox in Comiskey Park, a no-frills venue symbolic of his club's proletarian roots. Situated within smelling and spitting distance of the south side's slaughterhouses, Comiskey was constructed in only four months—on a former garbage dump site. What it lacked in glamour, however, it delivered in glitz. Later renovations included "the Monster," the world's first exploding scoreboard. Whenever a Sox player homered, the 130-foot techno-wonder unleashed a 32-second cacophony of sirens, horns, and fireworks.

The most infamous group ever to call this field home was made up of eight players—including legendary "Shoeless" Joe Jackson—known as the Black Sox. Accused of throwing the 1919 World Series against the Cincinnati Reds, their names became forever linked to baseball's most famous scandal. A trial jury returned a "not guilty" verdict, but baseball commissioner Judge Landis awarded his own form of justice: All Black Sox were banned for life from professional baseball.

The controversy still echoes, particularly over Shoeless Joe, so nicknamed for playing a game in socks after new shoes blistered his feet. Unlike his cohorts, who racked up poor hits, errors, and second-rate pitching, Jackson's performance in the "fixed" games was flawless, with a World Series record of 12 hits. Efforts to reinstate Jackson, who died in 1951, continue.

After decades of Series no-shows, fans feared that their boys faced similar banishment. But the Black Sox curse lifted in the 2005 World Series, when the Sox swept the Houston Astros to claim clean victory.

Comiskey Park shook off past ghosts as well. The old structure was retired in 1990, and a slick new Comiskey (since renamed U. S. Cellular Field) debuted across the street, where today's greats play by the rules.

Chicago White Sox:

Major leaguers whose claims to fame include the Black Sox scandal of 1919 and a Series sweep over the Houston Astros 86 years later.

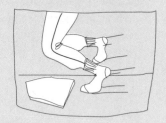

illinois
. . . fancy dancing fuels the fans

"Chief, Chief, Chief, Chief . . ." Chanting begins, slow but insistent, and soon spreads like wildfire through the stands, its cadence and volume flamed by the voices of Illini faithful focused on a familiar ritual.

It's halftime at a University of Illinois home football or basketball game, and fans are signaling their mascot, Chief Illiniwek—or The Chief, as he's known in collegiate circles. On cue the Marching Illini Band forms a block *I*, and Chief Illiniwek slips stealthily into a center row. He emerges at midfield, or midcourt, and for the next four minutes the crowd forgets the score.

In the traditional dress of the Plains Indians, the Chief performs an authentic and studied "fancy dance" associated with Native American celebrations. What begins with a basic double step soon escalates to intricate footwork, dizzying spins, split jumps, and high kicks. Thousands of clapping hands reach a crescendo as spectators spring to their feet. They remain standing for the Chief's finale: With arms folded high on his chest, he is motionless as the band plays "Hail to the Orange," the University's alma mater.

Chief Illiniwek and his dance have symbolized the University and its athletic teams since 1926. Like Illinois itself, the Chief is named for the native Algonquin tribe who called themselves *Illiniwek*, meaning

Chief Illiniwek:

Longtime mascot of the University of Illinois sports teams.

"men." And although subject to recent controversy, the Chief has been long endorsed by Native American descendents.

Criteria established in 1930 by A. Webber Borchers, the second Chief Illiniwek, still define this legendary mascot: Candidates must know University history, understand the significance of Indian dancing, be Eagle Scouts, and "never let the Illiniwek tradition become clownish or ludicrous."

illinois
...politicians are often unlawful

Forget red states and blue states. The enduring symbol of Illinois politics is the shoe box. Ever since former secretary of state Paul Powell died in 1970, leaving $800,000 of suspicious origin stashed in shoe boxes in his hotel room, the state has been known for having more than its share of . . . uh, interesting politicians.

Not all are swathed in scandal. Senator Everett Dirksen was a leading proponent of civil rights and best known for criticizing government spending by saying, "A billion here, a billion there, and pretty soon it adds up to real money." (Never mind that Dirksen apparently never said these exact words. When quizzed about it years later, the legislator admitted that a reporter had misquoted him but he liked the interpretation and stuck with it.) Illinois governor Adlai Stevenson II failed twice to wrest the presidency from Dwight D. Eisenhower. But as a United Nations ambassador from 1961 to 1965, he was the world's most insistent voice for disarmament.

Still, bad apples make better stories, and the Land of Lincoln has a long-running, nationwide reputation for being ethically challenged. Governor Otto Kerner went to jail for accepting racetrack bribes. Chicago mayor Richard Daley became a cliché for a boss-controlled political machine. Governor George Ryan's tenure was tainted with criminal indictments.

Colorful Politicians:

Illinois' larger-than-life political figures, many of whom walk the line between saints and scoundrels.

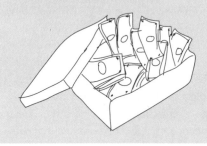

Powell never earned a state salary of more than $30,000 per year over his 35-year career as a public servant. Yet this man of humble origins and meager means amassed an estate that, when settled in 1978, was worth $4.6 million—including nearly $1 million in racetrack stock.

Illinoisans have a weird sense of pride in recounting such stories of corruption. But then, Illinois politics are complicated from the get-go. No other state has more units of government than the Prairie State, which has 102 counties, nearly 1,300 cities and villages, and more than 1,400 townships. Add at least 2,500 special districts that oversee airports, libraries, parks, and more than 950 school districts. That's lots of soap boxes, if not shoe boxes.

illinois
. . . the world turns your way

What on earth do Shredded Wheat cereal, Pabst Blue Ribbon beer, Juicy Fruit gum, and a Ferris wheel have in common?

One World's Fair launched them all—along with Cracker Jacks, the Midway, automatic dishwashers, Aunt Jemima pancake mix, and vertical files. Hosted by Chicago in 1893 to celebrate the 400th anniversary of Columbus's discovery of America, the six-month, $17 million Columbian Exposition got the globe spinning with revolutionary products, inventions, and ideas.

Of the 27 million visitors, few could imagine the marvels waiting along a 1.3-mile strip in Jackson Park. Hearing an orchestra as it played, that very moment, in New York City via a long-distance telephone! Watching moving pictures on Thomas Edison's Kineto-scope! Seeing a hydrogen-filled balloon carry folks 1,000 feet above the Midway! Circling for 20 minutes in a plush, wood-paneled Ferris wheel car!

As they marveled at the sights, fairgoers might have spotted some of the world's brightest souls: Buffalo Bill, Clarence Darrow, George Westinghouse, Susan B. Anthony, and Jane Addams.

The exposition even occupied a community of its own, consisting of 200 sparkling structures and dubbed the White City. Built in the simple Beaux Arts style, a radical departure from ornate Victorian, the Manu-

factures and Liberal Arts Building alone was big enough to house the U.S. Capitol, the Great Pyramid of Giza, Winchester Cathedral, Madison Square Garden, and St. Paul's Cathedral—all at once. The world's largest building at the time, this structure spanned 44 acres and stood 19 stories high.

A black cloud hung over the White City, however. With one gleaming exception, today's Chicago Museum of Science and Industry, structures were either dismantled or destroyed in a July 1894 fire.

Alongside the modern-day success stories rooted in the fair were a number of one-hit wonders, including a giant U.S. map made from pickles, a knight on horseback sculpted from prunes, and a suspension bridge built of soap.

Columbian Exposition:

The 1893 Chicago World's Fair, which celebrated the 400th anniversary of Columbus's discovery of America.

illinois

...futures lie in the pits

Arms flail frantically; faces go from grimaces to grins—and back—in seconds; and voices crescendo and crash at random. Men and a handful of women, all dressed in wild-colored jackets, move about the floor in manic patterns, pausing only to check computer screens, shout into headsets, or pitch pieces of paper.

If this was anyplace but West Jackson Street in the Windy City, you'd swear you had descended to a madhouse. But in the grain pit of the Chicago Board of Trade (CBOT) building, it's just another day at the office.

Herein throbs the heart of America's agricultural industry, where half the nation's commodities are traded: soybeans and soybean oil, pork bellies, grain, corn, wheat, silver, oats, barley, iced broilers (frozen chickens), stocks, and bonds. Deals are sealed by futures contracts—promises to buy or sell and receive or deliver a particular commodity on a set date.

Pumping adrenaline through the pit are traders, those of the thrashing body parts, who play the market according to buy or sell orders. Mandates arrive from their customers, any one of about 3,600 CBOT members, including bankers, millers, elevator owners, and cooperative farm groups. And what happens in the pit never stays in the pit. Prices here are recorded within seconds, and these intricate trader/customer interactions—beamed worldwide—determine global commodity prices.

It all started in 1830, when a group of enterprising Chicago merchants gathered to devise a standardized way to sell farm products from a central U.S. spot. Although many may have wrung their hands over the markets since, the CBOT has withstood the test of time. Reduced to ashes by the 1871 Chicago Fire, it reopened two weeks later in a temporary wooden structure called the Wigwam. The "pit" also rose in the face of the Wall Street panic of 1873, Great Depression, and October 1987 stock market crash. All are past indicators that futures rest in good, albeit somewhat busy, hands.

See all the pit action for yourself from the safety of the CBOT observation area. Check out www.cbot.com for more information.

Commodity Trading:

Manic buying and selling of commodities from the Chicago Board of Trade "grain pit" that determines market prices worldwide.

22

illinois
...ears have kernels

Row after row of corn plants march across the Illinois horizon until they seem to vanish in the heat vapors. On summer days when the humidity is high and the moisture plentiful, old-timers say you can hear the green shoots growing. A good crop is always "knee-high by the Fourth of July." By the dog days of August, the tassels are nodding, silks have turned brown under the summer sun, and ears have grown heavy in the husk.

Illinois is the Corn Belt. More than 12 million acres were planted in the state's rich soils in 2005, and there's a lot more to an ear than cornflakes. Corn feeds the animals that fill the meat and milk cases. Cornstarch is used in everything from adhesives to aspirin. Corn syrup sweetens soft drinks. Illinois corn processors squeeze more than half the ethanol produced in the United States. Consumers buy baby blankets, biodegradable trash bags, carpets, cat litter—even a skunk-odor remover—made from corn. Specialty corns like popcorn, blue corn, and Indian corn are also raised in Illinois.

The hot, buttery corn that ends up on your dinner plate is a cousin to these dent-type varieties. More than 50 years ago, a University of Illinois corn geneticist named John Laughnan began to wonder why some kernels were shriveled and shrunken. He discovered a gene that makes some corn

Corn:

Illinois' largest crop, which is grown for feed, fuel, and food.

"sweet," and over time varieties of corn were bred to be sweeter and more tender, have a better shelf life, and resist diseases. Protecting the crop from critters is another matter. Each summer gardeners wage war against raccoon bandits. Burrus Hybrids, an Arenzville-based seed company, markets its sweet-corn selections under the tongue-in-cheek label "Coon's Choice."

The period of peak freshness for sweet corn is measured in minutes, not hours or days. The best corn is simply the freshest corn. August brings festivals honoring the golden crop to the towns of Hoopeston and Mendota. Learn more about corn at the Chicago Museum of Science and Industry's farm exhibit. For more information, visit www.msichicago.org and www.ilcorn.org.

illinois
. . . blood boils red or blue

The Hatfields and McCoys have nothing on Illinois' grudge matches, long-running and long-winded feuds lived out in living rooms and sports bars, on fields, over airwaves, in newspapers, and across backyard fences. You can cross the state's Mason-Dixon line (north-south Interstate 55) and find yourself in enemy territory or, just as easily, land on the wrong side of a cornfield, sidewalk, or kitchen table.

Black or white, but no gray. When the boys of summer play at Wrigley Field or Busch Stadium, you're either Chicago Cubs blue or St. Louis Cardinals red. True colors date to the old days, when these two were the farthest west of all major league teams. Geography, along with strong broadcasting traditions—Cardinals commanded radio and Cubs controlled television—spawned loyalties that define generations.

Listen to Cubbies and Cards enthusiasts debate all-time greats, and you'll go to extra innings. Cubs fans toss out Don Cardwell, Ferguson Jenkins, Ryne Sandburg, and Mark Grace. The Cardinals faithful pitch Bob Gibson, Lou Brock, Stan Musial, and Ozzie Smith. Both camps still regale 1998's home-run slugfest between Mark McGwire and Sammy Sosa. "Reds" are quick to mention that McGwire won with 70 homers in a single season to Sosa's 66. "Blues" counter that Slammin' Sammy was the runaway favorite for the league's MVP.

Cubs vs. Cardinals:

A long-running interstate baseball feud that divides friends, families, and fans.

History records a fair number of defectors—players traded, willingly or not, to the other side. But none converted more vocally than legendary broadcaster Harry Caray. From 1954 to 1969, "downstate" radios blasted Caray's trademark "Holy cow!" and "It might be, it could be . . . it is! A home run!" Thirteen years and a few moves later, Caray slid into Wrigley Field with "Cubs win! Cubs win!" and choruses of "Take Me Out to the Ball Game."

Fans share more than their claims to Caray. Both teams tout first-class corporate ownership (Anheuser-Busch in St. Louis and Tribune Company in Chicago), uniform logos that are among the league's oldest, and fervently loyal fans. Just don't expect these dueling diehards to admit it.

illinois

...nothing runs like a Deere

Long before the leaping-deer logo became a hip teenage trademark to wear to the mall, there was a plow that sliced through the prairie like a hot knife through butter. It all started in 1837 with one man's vision, rooted in the earth. John Deere—pioneer, inventor, and entrepreneur—revolutionized American agriculture by developing and marketing the world's first self-polishing steel plow.

Incorporated as Deere & Company in 1868, the business that came to bear John's name grew from a one-man blacksmith shop into a worldwide corporation that today does business in more than 160 countries and employs approximately 46,000 people. Headquartered in Moline, the company remains guided by Deere's principal that dependability means delivering what you promise.

The venerable two-cylinder tractors manufactured from 1923 to 1960 populated thousands of farms. Affectionately named "Johnny Poppers," these simple-to-repair tractors are now prized by collectors. And the company continues to break new ground. Deere's 9860 STS combine chews through corn stalks 12 rows at a time, holds 300 bushels of corn, and unloads 3.3 bushels per second. At the beginning of the 20th century, it took four farmers to feed 10 people. Today such mechanics allow one U.S. farmer to produce enough food for 129 people.

See where Deere's dream began in Grand Detour at the John Deere Historic Site. Visit his home, the archeological site of his original blacksmith shop, and a reproduction of the shop. Along Moline's riverfront, near the site of Deere's first factory, the glass-sheathed John Deere Pavilion displays giant combines, tractors, and other descendants of the "plow that broke the prairie." Load up on toys, caps, shoes, and sunglasses at the adjacent John Deere Store.

Also in Moline, step back in time at the John Deere Collectors Center, a 1950s-era dealership where mechanics restore tractors and farmers swap tales. Visitors can also tour two Deere family homes and gardens a few blocks south of downtown. For more information, visit www.deere.com and www.johndeerepavilion.com.

Deere, John:

The pioneer plowmaker whose invention transformed the prairie into the world's breadbasket.

illinois
. . . caramel apples are a food group

An apple a day might keep the doctor away, but in the central Illinois community of Decatur, triple-dipped caramel apples from Del's Popcorn Shop ooze new business for local dentists.

These sinfully sweet, sticky treats date to the 1950s, when former Popcorn Shop owner Del Barnett determined that the market was ripe for caramel apples. His pick? "Schoolboy" apples, named because their average size meant mothers wouldn't complain about paying for an apple that was too big for their kids to eat.

Customers bit, and Del's soon was hand-dipping about 100 caramel apples a day. Decades later the same small confectionery washes, dips, rolls, dries, wraps, and bags up to 2,500 apples daily, many of which ship to customers worldwide. Choices include plain or nut (Del's grinds about 1,500 pounds of peanuts each season) and single-, double-, or triple-dipped.

Many Del's diehards claim that caramel lies at the core of the treat's success. The recipe, a closely guarded Popcorn Shop secret, yields a soft, rich concoction still made on-site daily.

Following a short, sweet season from Labor Day to Halloween, Del's customers trade caramel apples for another time-honored taste treat—Del's popcorn. Popped over an open flame using no oils or fats, kernels heat up in founder John Baldwin's "old and unimproved" popper, circa 1947. The contraption is pretty temperamental, too, and accepts only corn grown in central Illinois. Made-while-you-wait popcorn flavors include plain, cheese . . . and caramel, of course.

Taste for yourself! To order any Del's delicacy, visit www.delspopcorn.com.

Del's Caramel Apples:

Seasonal, hand-dipped treats made only in Decatur, but sold and shipped worldwide.

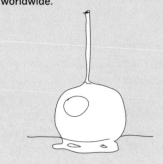

illinois
. . . business dumps from a skys-crapper

Because prairie life in the 1800s could be somewhat crude, folks sought convenience wherever they could find it. And in the central Illinois town of Gays, they looked no further than the seat of their pants.

Like their neighbors statewide, Gays' residents were all too familiar with conducting "business" in outhouses, 4-by-7-foot facilities with no windows, heat, or electric light. "Meetings" always concluded with a quick swipe of newspaper or catalog pages and an even quicker dash to escape decidedly ripe odors.

No wonder, then, that when Gays businessman Samuel Gammill built a double-decker structure in 1869, folks cheered the elevation of outhouse standards. Attached to a building that housed Gammill's first-floor general store and an upstairs hotel, the two-story "tower" spared his guests the indignity of coming downstairs and walking through the store, thus announcing their movements to everyone. Space was ample, too, with each level boasting a two-seater/stander.

Much to the relief of top and bottom poopers, Gammill paid close attention to placement. A lower-level pit, situated behind a false wall, safely received "gifts" that fell from above.

Double-Decker Outhouse:

A two-story facility erected in Gays, Illinois, and the oldest of its kind in existence.

The general store/hotel building no longer stands, but instead of flushing its attachment, townsfolk moved the double-decker to its present spot, just north of Gays' grain elevator along Route 16. Today the "skyscrapper" in this 250-person burg claims the undisputed distinction of being the oldest structure of its type in existence. It's also an official state tourist stop. Each year thousands of curiosity-seekers simply can't pass up the opportunity to snap a photo at one of Illinois' most unique rest stops.

When you visit, focus and shoot all you want. Just don't plan on doing any business.

illinois

...the state is divided

No one really knows when Chicago seceded from the rest of the state. But everyone who lives in Illinois knows that a split exists that all but defies definition.

The term *downstate* is generally understood to mean all of Illinois not encompassed by Chicago and its suburbs or surrounding counties. For some Illinoisans, downstate begins at the southwest city limits of Chicago. Others would argue that it is any area south of Interstate 80 or Bloomington or Decatur.

Even the *down* in *downstate* is a misnomer. "I live downstate" could mean you live in Rockford or Moline, which are actually west of Chicago.

Fact is, this arbitrary Mason-Dixon line isn't on any map because it is more a state of mind than an issue of geography. Chicago is perceived as big-city busy, noisy, crowded, and filled with ethnic diversity. Downstate is considered laid-back, quiet, sparsely populated, and filled with farm folk.

At least half the state's population does live in Chicagoland, but such broad generalities ignore the city's agrarian roots. Meatpacking and agricultural machinery made the city's early economy; livestock and grain still trade throughout the world based on Chicago prices. One of the premier high schools in the Chicago area emphasizes agricultural studies. And Chicago has become known as one of the "greenest" cities in America, with lush parks and rooftop gardens sprouting like weeds.

In its defense, downstate isn't lacking culture. It is the hub for state policy-making and for Illinois' university system. Less than 2 percent of the population farm, and those who do are mostly college educated. Some of the most astounding architecture and art in Illinois can be found downstate.

Still, downstaters are often convinced that Chicago steals their highway money and siphons off education dollars. Chicagoans sometimes consider downstate to be nothing but corn and cows. The truth lies somewhere in between. Illinois is both urban and rural, and the controversy this combination stirs up gives the state a hearty soul.

Downstate:

Almost anywhere in Illinois but Chicago proper.

CHICAGO

illinois

... playing in the dirt becomes a work of art

From the air, the old strip mine outside Ottawa has the makings of a real, live creature feature. Giant earthen mounds molded into the shapes of a turtle, a snake, a catfish, a frog, and a water-striding spider leap from the landscape.

Considered the most ambitious outdoor sculpture since Mount Rushmore, the Effigy Tumuli earthworks within Buffalo Rock State Park in LaSalle County are the largest artwork of their kind in the world.

Inspired by Native American effigy mounds, artist Michael Heizer created the larger-than-life critters with heavy construction equipment after being commissioned in 1983 to reclaim the land. With a 1.5-mile-long bluff as the canvas, Heizer's 300-acre "gallery" allows visitors to gaze upon the art from a distance and then walk all over the sculptures to experience and understand them. Bring your hiking boots; the snake alone is 2,070 feet long.

Effigy mounds were first made by prehistoric Woodland Indians in this region more than a thousand years ago. Their animal, human, and geometric shapes were usually used as temple platforms or as burial mounds, called *tumuli*. Heizer, who published a book in 1990 on his mound-building efforts, calls Effigy Tumuli a "contemporary artwork that ties together themes of envi-

Effigy Tumuli:

Contemporary artwork created with ancient mound-building techniques to reclaim strip-mined land.

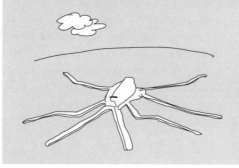

ronmentalism, Native American ethnography and animistic mysticism."

Before the project the land was barren, sterile, and useless—a moonscape polluted with the caustic spoils of the coal-mining process. The land was donated to the state of Illinois for the creative reclamation project by the Ottawa Silica Company.

Buffalo Rock State Park is located about 2 miles west of Ottawa. For more information, call (815) 433–2220.

illinois
...cheesecake means calories

The first creamy bite is sublime. The second is sinful. An entire slice of Eli's Cheesecake is pure decadence. This dreamy bit of heaven has been Chicago's top dessert since 1977.

Don't confuse it with New York– or French-style cheesecake. It is a unique Chicago-style version that bakes up a little thicker than other popular varieties and has a firm outside and creamy inside atop a prebaked butter/shortbread-cookie crust. The recipe relies on wholesome, simple ingredients: cream cheese, sugar, eggs, sour cream, vanilla, and salt, with no preservatives.

Purists go for the original plain cheesecake. But there's a long list of calorie-laden options. Try the Caramel-Nougat with Snickers specialty: caramel nougat cheesecake packed with soft caramel candy, topped by layers of chocolate ganache, chocolate mousse, caramel whipped cream, and more peanuts and chocolate.

At the company's 62,000-square-foot state-of-the-art bakery in northwest Chicago, some 25,000 cheesecakes march out of the tunnel oven each day. A retail store and dessert cafe are also located at the bakery. Eli's Cheesecake-to-Go at O'Hare airport lets you indulge one last time before takeoff.

Eli Schulman didn't start out to be the cheesecake king. He and his wife, Esther,

Eli's Cheesecake:

A rich, creamy legend that has grown from Chicago's most famous dessert to a national craving.

simply wanted to create a signature dessert for their Chicago restaurant, Eli's the Place for Steak, a hangout for movie and television stars. Eli spent several weeks coming up with the recipe, and it wasn't long before he was producing rich and creamy cheesecakes not only for his business, but for other restaurants and retail outlets as well.

The Schulman family still maintains the business, which is the largest specialty cheesecake bakery in the country. Their cheesecakes are sold in all 50 states and around the world, and there's even an Eli's fan club—a sure sign of sweet success. For more information, visit www.elicheesecake.com.

illinois

... parties last 'til the cows come home wearing ribbons

Among the coolest ways to spend a dog day of summer (or a dog night, for that matter) is at any of Illinois' 102 hot spots—county fairs.

Some partiers pull in with dairy cows in tow, each bovine's tail carefully braided and sprayed and hair freshly clipped. Others lug what could be the county's longest snake cucumber, or the area's flakiest piecrust. Fair Queen wannabes primp and pose, and food vendors saturate the deep-fat fryers.

And just as many come to see the cows, cucumbers, crusts, carnies, queens, and countless other characters and curiosities flaunted at every turn.

Direct offshoots of the state's agrarian roots, county fairs have long fueled the competitive nature of farm folks. Yester-year's promos encouraged farmers and their wives to "do a better job on your own farms . . . by seeing how other people pro-duce superior livestock and preserves." To this day neighbors might shake hands on the midway, but once inside the livestock barn or exhibit hall, they beat a path to sep-arate stalls. Seeking a blue ribbon, it seems, is akin to the quest for the Holy Grail.

You can take the farm out of the fair—4-H lambs and patch quilts share billing with demolition derbies and rock bands—but a sameness nevertheless sticks like cotton candy. In counties from Boone in the north to Massac way down south, days can go to the hogs, pigs, cows, and sheep, but nights belong to the midway. Within this honky-tonk heaven, teens travel in packs, with guys tossing rings to win huge stuffed teddy bears for gals and couples pairing off for thrill rides like the Zipper, Sizzler, and Avalanche.

Night and day, fairgoers of all ages relish concoctions you'll never find on the food pyramid. Name it, and you'll likely find it deep-fried and served on a stick: cheese, mushrooms, pickles, candy bars, corn dogs. All taste best, of course, washed down with a sublimely sweet lemon shake-up.

Fairs:

Summertime festivals that celebrate the best of agriculture, deep-fried food, friendship, and good old-fashioned fun.

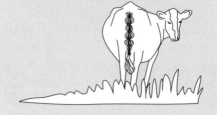

illinois
...farms are up and growing

From the air Illinois looks like a patchwork quilt stitched together into regular geometric shapes. The tidy piecework goes all the way back to a 1785 land survey that neatly carved the state into 6-mile-square townships and divided each township into 36 one-mile-square sections. Over time, rows of roads and property lines defined the grid and farmsteads, churches, and towns accumulated at the corners.

Detour from today's monotonous interstate highways to find the back roads that reveal Illinois' true character. White farmhouses with wide front porches, massive red barns, and towering cement silos appear around each bend in postcard-pretty splendor. Between the corn and soybean fields, cattle graze upon green fescue pastures. Roadside placards point to apple and peach orchards. Bumper stickers on pickup trucks proclaim, "Farming is everyone's bread and butter."

Illinois farms cover more than 28 million acres—nearly 80 percent of the state's total land area. The state's agriculture industry employs nearly one million people, and marketing the commodities grown here generates more than $9 billion annually. Billions more flow into the state's economy from agriculture-related industries, such as equipment manufacturing. More than 950 food-manufacturing companies make food processing the state's number-one manufacturing activity, adding approximately $13.4 billion annually to the value of Illinois' agricultural commodities.

Today there are only 76,000 farmers in the state, down from 164,000 in 1959. During the same time period, the size of the average farm doubled as sophisticated technology replaced manual labor. Satellites and global positioning systems now automatically guide tractors and combines through fields. The same space-age technology can pinpoint the location of a single cow by a computer chip ear tag.

More than 7,200 Illinois farms have been classified as "Centennial Farms," owned by the same family for at least 100 years. Hard but wholesome work, farming remains the fabric that binds this state together.

Farms:

Stalwart, enduring agricultural enterprises that are the backbone of Illinois' economy.

illinois
. . . big wheels keep on turning

The big wheel spins round and round. Every corner of the carnival whirls with light and jumps with sound. Sweethearts clasp hands, sneak kisses, and gasp as the gondola teeters to a stop at the top of a twinkling world.

No amusement park is complete without the magic of a Ferris wheel, an attraction more thrilling than scary. Attribute the ride's popularity to the ingenuity of the Eli Bridge Company, which has been building Ferris wheels in the village of Jacksonville since the early 1900s.

European and Oriental cultures had enjoyed pleasure wheels for centuries. But Illinoisan George Washington Gale Ferris Jr., an engineer and native of Galesburg, stunned the world when he built an enormous wheel for the 1893 Columbian Exposition in Chicago. It towered 265 feet above the fairgrounds, its 125-foot wheel turning on a 56-ton axle that was the largest piece of steel ever forged.

Bridge builder William Sullivan was one of the 1.5 million people willing to pay 50 cents to enjoy two revolutions on Ferris's wheel. Captivated by the experience, Sullivan came home to western Illinois determined to literally reinvent the wheel by downsizing it and making it portable. His first effort was a 45-foot-tall wheel powered by a small gasoline engine, with 12 buggy seats.

Ferris Wheel:

Popular amusement ride built in Illinois that provides hometown fun.

When Sullivan decided to mass produce his version, he incorporated the Eli Bridge Company. (Skeptical company shareholders suggested that he not forget his original trade. The rest of the company name comes from Sullivan's favorite expression, "Get there, Eli," which in today's vernacular would be "Get 'er done.") The prototype still stands before the family-owned factory as a monument.

The company has never erected a bridge. But if you've ever ridden a Ferris wheel, chances are good that it was a "Big Eli." The largest model stretches 67 feet skyward and carries 48 passengers; the smallest is the six-seat Lil' Wheel. The company also manufactures a popular nonwheel, double-rotation ride called The Scrambler, as well as a SpiderMania ride.

illinois
. . . gardens go to the dogs

Don't count on these mutts as best friends. They may not bite, but they won't shake paws, play fetch, or roll over, either.

They know only one command: "Stay." Standing perfectly still, the dogs mirror passersby who stop mid-stride to gaze at the breed's ornamental eyebrows; curved horns; long, hairy ears; large, luminous eyes; and ferocious mouths.

Meet Robert Allerton Park's 22 Chinese fu dogs, planted in 1932 in the park's Fu Dog Garden, part of a 6,000-acre country estate located in central Illinois near Monticello. Common in Asian art, these striking lapis-lazuli blue ceramic sculptures combine features of Pekingese pugs and long-haired lion dogs—an interesting parentage, to be sure. At Allerton, as in their native land, they are tasked with warding off demon spirits.

Identical except for small spots and minute curves in ears and tails, these pups are among the last sights you'd expect would sprout from prairie soil. But when Robert Allerton began the decades-long process of cultivating his property in 1900, the "wow" factor was exactly what he wanted. His estate, which he called The Farms, included formal gardens, an intricately landscaped park dotted with fine art and more than 100 sculptures from around the world, and a 30-room manor modeled after England's Hamm House. The fantastically wealthy son of livestock baron Samuel Allerton, Robert

Fu Dogs:

Intricately carved ceramic sculptures that awe visitors and protect the gardens of Monticello's Robert Allerton Park.

studied art in Europe and brought his international flair and education back to the heartland.

Allerton traveled the world with his adopted son, John Gregg, and in 1946 donated his woodland property to the University of Illinois as a conservation area for education, recreation, and research. This extensive gift included 3,775 acres of fertile farmland.

Each year thousands visit Allerton Park's magnificent menagerie where, in addition to fu dogs, an assortment of sphinxes, lions, Chinese goldfish, and Japanese guardian fish make their homes.

Want to go to the dogs? You'll find upcoming events listed on Allerton's Web site: www.allerton.uiuc.edu.

illinois

...trees grow sweeter with age

There's sap in them-there tall trees, and it's not just your typical run-of-the-trunk sweet stuff. To the makers of legendary Funks Grove Pure Maple Sirup, it's akin to liquid gold.

Thousands of maple trees are rooted within Funks Grove, a central Illinois wide spot in the woods. They're among the state's oldest—many top 500 years—and paleo-botanists believe that the grove itself may date to 2500 B.C. Each spring when temperatures tease, elders and their offspring yield buckets of sap that sweeten pancake stacks worldwide.

Tapping trickles back to 1824, when Isaac and Cassandra Funk settled in the area that would later bear their name. On an estate that eventually spanned 25,000 acres of farmland, they raised 10 children. Two of the older Funk sons made sirup for the family, assuming the chore for their father, who served in the Illinois Senate and was a close friend to Abraham Lincoln.

The family tradition stayed as thick as molasses, even after Isaac and Cassandra died (within three hours of each other) in 1865. Their grandson, Arthur Funk, opened the first commercial sirup farm at Funks Grove in 1891 and sold his product for $1.00 per gallon. Fourth-generation Funks now manage 6,500 taps and produce about 1,600 gallons of sirup a year. Prices fluctu-

ate with fuel and labor costs but generally hover around $39 per gallon. Sirup was still sold from the front porch of the original Funk home until 1988, when a new sugar house was constructed.

Why *sirup* with an *i?* That particular tradition respects the wishes of Hazel Funk Holmes, granddaughter of Isaac, who took over the operation in the early 1920s and eventually owned the land. Hazel's will, which provided for a trust to protect the timber and farmland, included a caveat: that *sirup—Merriam-Webster's* preferred spelling at the time—always stick with its *i*.

Tickle your taste buds with a visit to Funks Grove, or order online at www.funkspure maplesirup.com.

Funks Grove Pure Maple Sirup:

A fourth-generation family-produced sirup made with sap from some of Illinois' oldest maple trees.

illinois

...miners make their mark

Scratch the surface in northwest Illinois and find treasure. The rugged bluffs hold lead deposits that sparked the nation's first mineral rush in the late 1820s. The town of Galena is named for the ore and survives seemingly untouched by time, making it one of the most popular tourist destinations in Illinois.

In its heyday, the business district thrived and mining barons and steamboat captains built grand homes. But the boom fizzled and progress bypassed Galena, leaving the town to sleep like Rip van Winkle until preservationists discovered it more than a century later. Today most of the town is listed on the National Register of Historic Places.

Main Street remains narrow, as it was in the mid-1800s. Its buildings, like finely dressed old ladies, shelter specialty shops, galleries, candy stores, and restaurants. A hillside warren of restored redbrick mansions, elaborate Victorian cottages, and white-spired churches rises above Main Street and the Galena River, a shallow Mississippi River tributary.

Pick up a walking-tour map east of the river at the Old Train Depot, now a visitor center. Stay in one of the many historic homes born again as bed-and-breakfasts. The oldest operating post office in the United States still processes mail downtown. Nearby, the restored DeSoto Hotel, her-

alded in the 1850s as the finest west of New York City, fills most of a block. On the southeast edge of town, you'll find the 1865 brick home of Ulysses S. Grant, one of nine Civil War generals who hailed from Galena.

Climb the steps from Main Street to Prospect Street to get a bird's-eye view of the village. Untouched by Ice Age glaciers, this corner of Illinois seems almost mountainous by Midwest standards. Charles Mound and Scales Mound, the highest points in Illinois, can be viewed from this overlook. Get above it all in a hot-air balloon or go underground and visit Vinegar Hill Lead Mine, the only lead mine in Illinois open for tours.

For more information, visit www.galena.org.

Galena:

A step-back-in-time town that has become one of Illinois' most popular tourist destinations.

illinois
... there's a mob scene

If Illinois has a vice, it is the pulp glorification of gangsters. Al Capone and his peers loom as large in popular culture as they did in the era of Prohibition. Chicago is known far and wide as "gangsterland," and downstate is no less tarnished thanks to southern Illinois bootleggers like Charlie Birger and his rivals, the Shelton Brothers Gang.

When Congress enacted the Volstead Act in 1919, making the manufacture and sale of alcoholic beverages illegal, the peddling of bootlegged beer and liquor in Chicago became a $30-million-a-year business. Capone, aka "Scarface," was soon Public Enemy Number One. He became a household name after the 1929 St. Valentine's Day Massacre, a notorious underworld slaying in which five men disguised as police officers gunned down seven members of Bugs Moran's gang. Capone's heyday from 1926 to 1931 saw 418 gangland slayings.

FBI agent Eliot Ness and his handpicked Bureau agents, "The Untouchables," gave the world a good story, even before actor Robert Stack recreated the epic beer wars each week in a TV series and Kevin Costner became Ness on the silver screen. Capone was convicted of tax evasion in 1931, only to leave Chicago to the likes of notorious bank robber John Dillinger and syndicate boss Sam Giancana.

In the midst of all this mayhem, cartoonist Chester Gould created a gumshoe named

Gangsters:

Big-time bad boys who flourished in Illinois during Prohibition and beyond.

Dick Tracy. "I decided if the police couldn't catch the gangsters, I'd create a fellow who could," Gould said. His *Chicago Tribune* comic strip—in which characters like Pruneface, Flattop, and Putty Puss mimicked real-life bad guys—reverberated with an edgy public fed up with machine-gun warfare.

Over the years Tracy sent plenty of rogues to the slammer using space-age technology like wrist radios. Learn how the ageless hero continues to make the world safe for democracy at a museum in Gould's hometown of Woodstock, which also hosts Dick Tracy Days in late June. To fit in, remember to wear a yellow fedora. For more information, visit www.chestergould.org.

illinois
. . . the gods are gardeners

South of Equality in southeastern Illinois, country back roads spiral and climb to the Garden of the Gods Recreation Area, part of the Shawnee National Forest. This hilly landscape seems worlds away from the flat farmlands usually associated with the Prairie State.

Eons ago the great ice sheets that smoothed out the upper Midwest stopped here, leaving a broken and heavily forested terrain. While travelers may be more familiar with Colorado's park of the same name, Illinois' version comes by its glorious title honestly. Even the gods of mythology would have approved of the sandstone bluffs rising above old-growth hardwoods, offering long blue vistas unique to the state.

A looping flagstone observation trail lets you hike the bluffs, where 320 million years ago the earth parted and huge volumes of sand and mud accumulated to form beautifully incised canyons and unusual rock formations that were eventually named by imaginative early explorers. A little scampering up some short, steep grades will lead you to views of the distinctive shapes of Camel Rock, Mushroom Rock, Devil's Smokestack, Anvil Rock, Table Rock, Monkey Face, and Chimney Rock.

Garden of the Gods:

A stunning federal wilderness area featuring ancient rock formations.

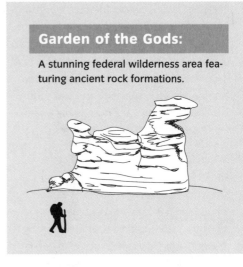

Garden of the Gods was established as a wilderness area by an act of Congress in 1990. No motorized vehicles or mechanized equipment are permitted in the 3,300-acre preserve. Nature does all the entertaining—birding, hiking, backpacking, horseback riding, hunting, fishing, canoeing, rappelling, camping, berry picking, cycling, swimming, spelunking, and photography opportunities attract true outdoorsmen. The area is filled with flora and fauna not found elsewhere in the state, and there are areas so wild that you'll swear you may be the first to have stepped foot in this heaven on earth. For more information, visit www.hardincountyil.org.

illinois
...you're stuck in the middle

Look around the tiny burg of Chestnut (population 250)—take in the bank, grain elevator, restaurant, corner store, barbershop, and four residential blocks—and you might feel you've found the middle of nowhere. Not so.

Where you're actually situated is someplace quite significant—Illinois' true geographic midpoint, as declared by the concrete monument in Chestnut Commons Park. The designation dates to 1992, when Gary Calvert, a native of nearby Pekin and a student at National College in South Dakota, visited the geographic center of the United States, near Castle Rock, South Dakota. Noting the site's appeal, Calvert—who was studying tourism at the time—concluded that a similar attraction would spark interest in his home state.

Starting with a somewhat off-kilter approach, he cut out an Illinois map, nailed it to a rafter in his basement, and traced down along a weighted fishing line hung from the northern city of Rockford. Calvert next flipped the map on its side and traced a bisecting line from Quincy, on the state's western border. Voilà: Chestnut.

After a University of Illinois survey team confirmed the results, Calvert presented his findings to Chestnut residents, who quickly rallied to form a volunteer Geocenter Committee. Working with a budget about the size of their town, they solicited design sketches from Illinois State University students, decided on a modest concrete pillar, and sold commemorative bricks to fund its completion.

The committee's clever publicity campaign featured Geocenter Dedication Day invitations from reigning "town dog" Crackers, a stray mutt adopted by Chestnut's grain elevator manager. Numerous state and national VIPs bit, including CBS's Bill Geist, who covered the June 13, 1993, ceremonies and featured the segment on *Sunday Morning*.

As Calvert envisioned, folks now come from all corners to center themselves in Chestnut. There, against a backdrop of flat farmland as far as the eye can see, the Geocenter is shadowed by the town's sole skyscraper—a towering grain elevator.

Geocenter:

A modest concrete pillar marking the geographic center of Illinois.

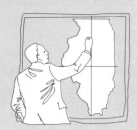

illinois
. . . cows host a real barn-burner

" . . . and when the cow kicked it over, she winked her eye and said, 'there'll be a hot time in the old town tonight.'" More than a century later, lyrics and legends still fan the flames. As the story goes, on the night of Sunday, October 8, 1871, a boot from Mrs. O'Leary's restless bovine tipped a lighted lantern in her barn, sparking the Great Chicago Fire.

Fueled by strong winds, flames atop O'Leary's blazing roof quickly started a crazy game of leapfrog, jumping north and east from structure to structure and mocking the Chicago River by crossing it twice. The inferno raged for 31 hours, quenched finally by a "miracle" rainstorm at 3:00 A.M. Tuesday. Reduced to ashes were 17,500 structures—ranging from shacks to mansions—and most of downtown Chicago. At least 300 residents died, and 90,000 were left homeless.

Chances are, however, that the much-maligned cow and its owner were merely unfortunate pawns in a predestined catastrophe. With its 40,000 wooden buildings, wooden warehouses stocked with inflammables, pine-block-paved streets, and rivers spanned by wooden bridges, the young city was a pyromaniac's fantasy. Even Mother Nature tossed on another log. Prior to the Great Fire, nary a raindrop had fallen on Chicago since July.

But from the rubble came rapid rebuilding and, eventually, fulfillment of the prophecy shared months after the disaster by author Alfred Sewell in his manuscript *The Great Calamity—Scenes, Incidents and Lessons of the Great Chicago Fire:* "The city . . . is already rising, like the Phoenix, from her ashes. And she will, we believe, be a better city as well as a greater one, than she was before her disaster."

Great Chicago Fire:

A citywide inferno that nearly destroyed Chicago in 1871.

illinois
...hippies are happening

Hey, man . . . hippies may have gotten lost in the 1960s, but you can find a shrine to them in Arcola (40 miles south of Champaign-Urbana). America's one and only Hippie Memorial takes the form of a metal sculpture that celebrates everything from flower power to populists.

Haight-Ashbury this isn't. Arcola is far from the bohemian enclaves of Greenwich Village and Berkeley and has no real connection to disaffected youth or the beat culture. What it had was Bob Moomaw, a local eccentric who worked as a tax assessor and railroad clerk. He was famous in his hometown for dealing with the pressures of working within the establishment by painting messages on the side of a building he owned. According to a 1993 *Chicago Tribune* story, the messages included things like "America you're turning into a nation of minimum-wage hamburger flippers. Rebel. Think for yourself. It works!"

Moomaw was also an artist who appreciated hippie culture. To construct a tribute to their ideals, he took iron rods and junk parts and welded together 62 feet of sculpture, one foot for each year of his life. The idea is that as his life passed, other people's junk stuck to him and made him what he was.

The first 26 feet of the memorial represent World War II, the Red Scare, and the

Hippie Memorial:

A monument that pays homage to the free-form hippie souls of the 1960s and 1970s.

hypocrisies of the 1950s. The middle section explodes with tie-dyed color to symbolize the Kennedy years, the coming of the hippies, and their break from small-town morality. Here are emblems like the Vulcan double-fingered greeting from *Star Trek* and a personalized license plate reading "WOODSTC." The last 18 feet of the monument are embedded with plain rusted scrap—Moomaw's statement about society settling into small-mindedness in the 1980s.

When Moomaw died in 1998, he bequeathed the whole metal heap to his friend Gus Kelsey, who refurbished it and got it installed next to Arcola's historic railroad station. At the center of the monument's stucco wall is a sandblasted peace sign that reads, "dedicated to hippies and hippies at heart, peace & love."

illinois
...a root is a hot commodity

You have to admire a crop that's been heralded as an aphrodisiac, a treatment for upper respiratory tract problems, and a massage salve for low back pain. It seems horseradish is more than just a spicy chaser to prime rib. This medical marvel is also a hot commodity for farmers in the Collinsville area, where at least 60 percent of the world's supply grows.

When Ice Age glaciers carved out this Mississippi River basin adjacent to St. Louis, Missouri, they left the soil rich in potash. This particular nutrient makes the perennial herb and member of the mustard family grow like crazy. Folks here see it as the king of condiments. The root is the centerpiece of the annual International Horseradish Festival, which attracts some 25,000 people each June. Events include a recipe contest, a root derby (with soapbox-style hot wheels), a root toss, and the crowning of Little Miss Horseradish.

Horseradish has nothing at all to do with horses, but its pungent flavor is capable of knocking one down. The bite and aroma of this thick, ornery root are almost absent until it is grated or ground. As the root cells are crushed, volatile oils are released and even the fumes become potent. Vinegar is used to stop this reaction and stabilize the heat in the final product.

German immigrants brought the root to the region in the late 1800s and passed the growing methods down through the generations. Locally, the J. R. Kelly Company purchases the crop from area farmers, marketing seven to eight million pounds of horseradish per year. The horseradish plant is not bothered by the pests that ravage other crops, but it requires a lot of hand labor during planting and harvesting.

Such work pays off beyond the dinner table. MIT scientists have found an enzyme in horseradish that removes a number of pollutants from wastewater. This gives a whole new meaning to being in hot water.

Horseradish:

A member of the mustard family that grows in Illinois and has medicinal, environmental, and gastronomic benefits.

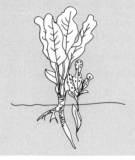

illinois

... a horseshoe is a dining delicacy

When in the Illinois state capital, forget BLTs, bologna, peanut butter, pastrami, and anything else you'd otherwise stack between two slices of bread. Instead, hunker down for a Horseshoe.

Concocted by two Leland Hotel chefs in 1928 and considered Springfield's signature sandwich, the calorie-laden Horseshoe is named for its appearance. Several slices of thick, toasted bread are topped with a horseshoe-shaped slab of ham steak or two large hamburger patties (the shoe); drizzled with creamy cheese sauce; circled with french fries (the nails); and delivered on a heated steak platter (the anvil). Those with slightly smaller appetites can sacrifice a slice of bread and opt for the Pony Shoe.

Through the decades area restaurants have pitched variations of the Horseshoe, introducing turkey, chicken, ham, Italian beef, and shrimp. The real ringer? Every chef claims his or her own cheese sauce recipe—and most aren't talking. But among published recipes, the following ingredients are common:

2 egg yolks
½ cup beer
2 T. butter
3 cups grated sharp cheddar or Colby
  cheese
1 tsp. Worcestershire sauce
¼ tsp. dry mustard

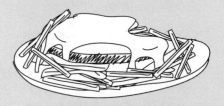

Horseshoe Sandwich:

An open-faced meat sandwich topped with cheese sauce and encircled by french fries.

½ tsp. salt
Dash of cayenne pepper

If this list has you hankering for a Horseshoe, beat the egg yolks and beer together and set aside. Melt the butter and cheese in a double boiler, then add the Worcestershire sauce and spices. Stirring constantly, gradually add the beer/egg mixture to the cheese mixture. Stir until the sauce thickens and begins to bubble.

illinois

. . . you're in "EL-e-noy"

Illinoisans have a language all their own. For example, ask for directions to Cairo, in the same way you would utter the Egyptian namesake, and you'll draw a knowing snicker. Locals says "k-AIR-oh" and the rest of the state tends to declare it "KA-roh," like the corn syrup found on the grocery shelf.

The tendency to pronounce words differently than the Europeans continues as you head northward in the state. Consider the village of Vienna, pronounced "VIE-an-nuh," and Versailles, which is said "Ver-SAILS."

Say you're searching for the road to Genoa. It seems only natural to articulate it with the accent on the first syllable—"GEN-o-wah." But stop at the gas station and the attendant will likely respond, "Oh, you mean 'gen-OH-wah'."

Put it down to linguistic laziness or just plain stubbornness, but in Illinois, Aledo is "uh-LEE-do" and Cordova, "Cor-DOE-vuh." Go ahead and sing about finding your way to San Jose, but you'll never find the 500-person Illinois community if you don't ask for "San-JOE-z." Rio, or "Rye-O" is not much of a party town, nor is Bourbonnais, despite being called "Bur-BON-ay." Those fluent in the state's diction know that New Berlin is expressed as "New BUR-lun" and you enunciate Athens like the word *eight*, or "AY-thens."

Illinois Pronunciation:

A way to tell natives from outsiders, depending on where they say they are going.

Perhaps the modulations are just a test, because much to the annoyance of residents, out-of-staters constantly boggle the state name by sneezing out something akin to "Ill-i-NOISE." This almost always causes a state of consternation. Go ahead and contradict the down-home speech pattern when referring to Illinois by removing the *s* and pronouncing a slightly breathless, very sophisticated "EL-e-noy."

illinois
... one guard shoots a lot of bull

The bull in a china shop has nothing on the Bull on a basketball court, a baseball field, a box of Wheaties cereal, television, magazine covers, clothing labels, athletic shoes, restaurant marquees, and the big screen with Bugs Bunny.

That's a lot of bull for anybody—even for Michael Jordan, a world-class athlete and legendary Chicago Bulls guard.

Basketball wasn't always a slam-dunk for this superstar. Seems Jordan didn't measure up as a 5-foot, 10-inch high school sophomore and was cut from the varsity squad. But a year later—and 4 inches taller—junior Jordan was back, averaging 29 points a game.

Next hoop: the North Carolina Tar Heels. As a college freshman Jordan won the 1981 national championship game with a jump shot. He racked up a title for his country as well, helping the United States' Olympic basketball team bring home the gold in 1984.

It was déjà vu that same year at the NBA draft, when pro teams looked right over Jordan's head. He was selected third by the Chicago Bulls, who tossed a few inches to the wind and took a chance on their future star.

The Chicago Stadium court soon crowned him king, and fans thrilled to the "Jordan-esque" style of play—body twists, slips,

speed, and the fantastic vertical leaps that earned Jordan the nickname "Air." His famous feet flew in custom-made Nike shoes, a new pair for each game.

Fans cried foul on October 6, 1993, when, after leading the Bulls to three consecutive NBA championships, Jordan announced that he would trade Nikes for baseball cleats. But after nearly two seasons of swings and misses in the minors, Jordan returned to play first with the Bulls (racking up another title three-peat) and then, after a brief second retirement, with the Washington Wizards.

When he retired for the third and final time in April 2003 at the age of 40, Jordan left the game he "never took for granted" with nothing but net: a total of 32,292 points—third highest in the NBA—and a 30.12 career point average, the league record.

Jordan, Michael:

World-class athlete best known as a guard for the Chicago Bulls.

illinois
...a capital capsizes

All roads once led to Kaskaskia, a booming cultural and commercial hub named the first Illinois territorial capital in 1809. Founded by French settlers in about 1703, the city was an important outpost in New France and, later, a springboard for westward explorations.

Today only a centuries-old bridge links this southwestern Illinois "ghost" island to the Missouri mainland, crossing the culprit responsible for Kaskaskia's demise—the Mississippi River. As if to add insult to injury, the isle is forever exiled from its home state, with shores reachable only via the bridge and only from the Missouri side.

Long trusted as a peacefully flowing neighbor, the Mississippi River had inexplicably shifted in its channel by 1870 and began devouring the strip of land between it and the smaller Kaskaskia River. A final gulp came on April 18, 1881, when the two waterways met in a massive union that flooded Kaskaskia and transformed the city from a small mainland peninsula to a desolate island.

Although it reached a peak population of 1,200, "new" Kaskaskia never rose to its predecessor's level. Due to floods and levee failures as recently as 1993, only about 20 residents now live on the island. A determined lot they are, however. Inhabitants gather to host a patriotic program every July 4 and an annual celebration the Sunday before Labor Day.

Cross to their isle, and you'll see the restored silver-and-bronze Kaskaskia Bell, given to the "old" community by King Louis XV in 1740 and housed in a shrine near the historic Immaculate Conception Church. The bell, 11 years older than the Liberty Bell, took two years to arrive from France and pealed the first chimes heard west of the Allegheny Mountains.

A hike to the nearby Fort Kaskaskia State Historic Site overlook affords a bird's-eye view of history's unrelenting flow—the convergence of the Mississippi and Kaskaskia Rivers. For more information, contact the Great River Road Interpretive Center at (573) 883-7097.

Kaskaskia:

Illinois' first territorial capital and only ghost island.

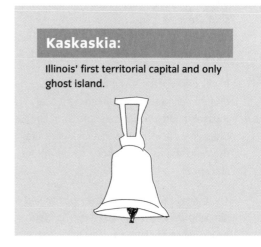

illinois
. . . one man stands as state symbol

At 6 feet, 4 inches, Abraham Lincoln cast a lengthy shadow. And his silhouette stretches particularly long across the state that "knew him when"—one where the "Land of Lincoln" slogan recognizes Abe's remarkable life and contributions and also identifies businesses, streets, colleges, communities, and license plates.

Lincoln landed smack dab mid-state in March 1830 as a gangly 21-year-old. He and his family built their cabin on a Sangamon River bluff near Decatur, a fledgling town that proved pivotal in Lincoln's political career. Decatur was the site of both his "Stump Speech," an early oratory on river navigation that grabbed the attention of area politicians, and the 1860 Illinois Republican Convention, where, under a 70-by-100-foot circus tent, Lincoln was first nominated for president as the "Railsplitter" candidate. (He formally accepted his party's nomination later that year at the National Replication Convention in Chicago.)

About 50 miles west, the towns of New Salem and Springfield saw "Honest Abe" as an Illinois General Assembly representative, successful lawyer, and member of the U.S. House of Representatives. Through his stirring antislavery discourses, delivered during the famed seven-town series of Lincoln-Douglas debates, townsfolk also gleaned glimpses of the man whose presidency would suffer the Civil War.

Land of Lincoln:

A state nickname that recognizes the contributions of Illinois' foremost former resident, Abraham Lincoln.

The places Lincoln lived for 23 years recall his homespun side. A re-created 1830s New Salem village introduces Lincoln as clerk and postmaster. Springfield sites include the only home he ever owned; his law office; and the Old State Capitol, which still echoes "A house divided against itself cannot stand." Lincoln's pew is preserved at First Presbyterian Church, and the family's account ledger is displayed at the Springfield Marine and Fire Insurance Company.

The 200,000-square-foot Abraham Lincoln Library and Museum, which houses the world's largest collection of documentary material related to the 16th president's life, opened in April 2005. For more information, call (217) 558–8882 or visit www.alincoln-library.com.

illinois

... counterculture lights the way

Chill out, man. LAVA® brand motion lamps live on in Illinois. The funky lamps that became a familiar fixture in college dorms and teenagers' bedrooms during the 1960s are just as popular today. And they're still made by the same Chicago manufacturer that took the concept from a haphazard invention to a cultural icon.

Liquid motion lamps came about when British engineer Edward Craven Walker found that by mixing a little of this and a little of that, you get globs of goo that undulate when heat is applied to the surrounding liquid. He worked on the concept for almost a decade before finally launching his Astro Lamp in 1963. Although Walker had moderate success, the design took off when two Illinois entrepreneurs spotted the light at a German trade show in 1965, acquired the U.S. patent rights, and branded the lamp with the LAVA name.

To this day Haggerty Enterprises, Inc., is the only manufacturer of official LAVA brand lamps. The cool thing about motion lamps is the amorphous blobs that hypnotically rise and fall in each lamp's globe. It takes two insoluble compounds of similar density to produce this effect. Temperature changes cause one of the compounds to become lighter than the other (so it floats) or heavier (so it sinks). Having compounds of similar densities allows the blobs to easily switch between rising and sinking.

LAVA® Brand Motion Lamp:

A uniquely hypnotic, blob-filled light that has been popular since the 1960s.

It sounds simple, but many have unsuccessfully tried to imitate the delicate balance of compounds, heat source, and globe size that makes the original LAVA brand lamp so groovy. The formula for the lamp remains a closely guarded secret, but who cares as long as there is peace, love, and LAVA.

For more information, visit www.lavaworld .com.

illinois
... lawn mowers go on parade

Meet the World Famous Lawn Rangers, a drill team that never lets the grass grow under its feet. Admittedly a few shoots shy of full sod, these Arcola-based goofs began performing in 1980 at the Arcola Broom-corn Festival Parade, held on the Saturday after Labor Day, and their annual antics soon spread faster than crabgrass in August.

Donning masks and cowboy hats, the Lawn Rangers take power mowers to artistic heights, parading and performing precision moves such as "Cross and Toss" and "Walk the Dog." They pause only long enough to grab an unsuspecting groupie from the crowd and honor him or her with a seat atop a mower fitted with a toilet bowl. Cheers abound as cameras click.

Many are called, yet few can master the supreme concentration, unflinching dedication, and hours of diligent practice required by this team. Rookie training camp, held for a full five minutes before a Ranger's first parade, is barely long enough to memorize the team motto: "You're only young once, but you're never too old to be immature."

For anyone doubting their claim to world fame, the Rangers tender these blades of truth: They have strutted their stuff alongside part-time member and national humor columnist Dave Barry and have edged into the national spotlight at Holiday and Fiesta Bowl parade performances.

Lawn Rangers:

A group of men who parade while pushing lawn mowers.

illinois

...good luck runs from a president's nose

Not even the nose knows precisely how it started, but since the late 1800s, visitors to the Lincoln family tomb in Springfield's Oak Ridge Cemetery have been reaching out and touching someone—or, rather, something: the proboscis of our 16th president.

Said snout, smoothed to a bright, shiny beacon lighting from Lincoln's otherwise dull face, graces a bronze bust sculpted by artist Gutzon Borglum of Mount Rushmore fame. Its placement on a pedestal near the 117-foot-tall granite tomb's entrance encourages the long-standing tradition of rubbing Honest Abe's nose for luck. No tiptoes required for adults; only a friendly boost needed for tots.

Assassinated on April 15, 1865, only six days after General Robert E. Lee surrendered his Confederate army to Union General Ulysses S. Grant, Abraham Lincoln was buried at Oak Ridge at the insistence of his wife, Mary Todd. His remains, and those of his son, William, who had died in 1862, were placed aboard a special train that traveled 1,700 miles from Washington, D.C., to Springfield, making 10 stops in 12 days.

Shortly after Lincoln's death, close friends and political associates, led by Illinois Governor Richard Oglesby, formed the National Lincoln Monument Association to raise money for a memorial. The $170,000 tomb, since reconstructed twice, was dedicated

on October 15, 1874. Burial chamber walls mark the location of the Lincoln family crypts—those of the president, first lady, and three of their four sons. (The oldest son rests in Arlington National Cemetery.)

Illinois' largest cemetery and the second-most-visited graveyard in the nation, Oak Ridge also is the final resting ground of famed poet Vachel Lindsay, four Illinois governors, and Lincoln law partner William Herndon. Although the cemetery is certainly appreciated for its historical significance, millions of luck-seeking visitors choose these 365 acres as a destination somewhat more temporary in nature.

For more information about the site, call the Oak Ridge Cemetery at (217) 782–2717 or go to www.visit-springfieldillinois.com.

Lincoln's Nose:

A supposed source of luck on the president's bronze bust at the Lincoln family tomb.

illinois

...the credit cards are smoking

The Magnificent Mile is Chicago's version of Beverly Hills' Rodeo Drive or New York's Fifth Avenue. This grand, wide boulevard is a 1-mile-long exclusive shopping extravaganza that stretches from the Chicago River north to Lake Shore Drive.

Bring your credit cards. All the famous names are here, from retail biggies like Bloomingdale's, Neiman Marcus, and Marshall Field's to prestigious boutiques like Tiffany & Co., Cartier, Giorgio Armani, and Salvatore Ferragamo.

Anchored by four- and five-diamond hotels and world-class dining establishments, the Mile attracts more than 22 million visitors each year. When folks aren't filling their shopping bags, they can admire the 40 parkway gardens that reflect Chicago's changing seasons along the strip or get a bird's-eye view of the city from the John Hancock Center, a 100-story skyscraper with an observation deck. The oldest building along the Mile is the castlelike Old Water Tower, built in 1869. It now serves as a visitor center and, as one of the few survivors of the 1871 Chicago Fire, symbolizes the city's resilience.

Michigan Avenue was widened in 1909 as part of a grand plan to transform it from an Indian trading post to a major commercial boulevard. Developers envisioned an

Magnificent Mile:

Chicago's mile-long ritzy shopping district centered along Michigan Avenue.

avenue that seemingly stretched to infinity, similar to the Champs Élysées in Paris. A bascule bridge modeled on the Pont Alexandre III in Paris was built to cross the Chicago River and create a gateway to the new district. Shop 'til you drop into sightseeing mode, then take in some more architectural splendor at the 30-story Wrigley building, with its towers and two-story clock, and the gothic Chicago Tribune Building.

For more information and a list of shops, visit www.themagnificentmile.com.

illinois
...shoppers read windows

At holiday time Santa's North Pole work-shop has nothing on the hustle and bustle surrounding 111 North State Street in downtown Chicago. And just as eagerly anticipated as the arrival of the jolly old soul himself is the annual unveiling of the windows lining this block, those of the venerable Marshall Field's State Street store.

Kids first pressed their noses to these panes in December 1897, enthralled with the toys cleverly flaunted by Arthur Fraiser, the store's display manager. Another picture-perfect idea came decades later, in 1946—the introduction of holiday story themes. When cold Lake Michigan winds blew and snow swirled, Chicagoans knew that the pouty storefront mannequins would soon be replaced by the likes of "Uncle Mistletoe," and Marshall Field's would tell another enchanting Christmas fairy tale, window by window.

A look inside this grand department store, founded by retailer Marshall Field in 1881 as a dry goods business, is still a bit like stepping into a storybook. You can take giddy looks down seven stories from the atrium railing; buy a bagful on Marshall Field's bargain day; or savor the warm elegance of the Walnut Room and its house specialties, chicken pot pie and apple pie.

Sweets have always been in season at the store with the long green awning and huge

Marshall Field's:

Chicago's State Street department store anchor, and home to traditions such as Christmas windows, the Walnut Room, and Frango Mints.

clock face. The one-and-only Frango Mints debuted at the Marshall Field's confectionary department in 1929, and today millions melt in mouths nationwide. Upstarts such as toffee crunch, raspberry, and coffee flavors have hopped into the mix since, but perennial bestseller chocolate mint never budges.

Renovated in 1992, this retail icon still sells tradition (along with all the treasures that hundreds of departments can hold) and draws thousands of faithful shoppers every holiday season. Should you visit the Walnut Room for lunch, request a table near the restaurant's giant Christmas tree. Look to the tippy-top; instead of an angel, you'll see Uncle Mistletoe. Listen carefully. He might have a story to tell.

illinois

...hamburgers create a fast-food dynasty

The famed McDonald's golden arches curve in countries worldwide, yet their true bent lies in Des Plaines, Illinois, site of founder Ray Kroc's first store. And a short order away in nearby Oak Park is Hamburger University—fast food's first training facility and the only institution of higher learning offering a degree in "hamburgerology."

The story began in 1954, when Kroc, then a distributor of five-spindled Multimixer milkshake makers, headed west from his Arlington Heights home to San Bernardino, California, to pay a visit to a pair of his biggest customers. Mac and Dick McDonald's speedy drive-in—a small, octagonal hamburger factory—slapped together its 15-cent signature sandwiches in assembly-line fashion and kept eight Multimixers churning continuously.

Awed by the restaurant's capabilities, Kroc convinced the McDonalds to franchise their concept. His return trip to Illinois, with exclusive contract in tow, signaled the launch of 51-year-old Kroc's second career as McDonald's Corporation founder.

Illinoisans boarded the burger wagon in June 1955 and never looked back. Opening-day revenue for the first McDonald's totaled $366.12. Customers relished the sight of its all-male crew flipping, mixing, serving, and cleaning. Decades later, more than 40 million customers a day "get up and get away" to McDonald's, convinced that they "deserve a break." And for more than half the country's population, the respite lies within a few miles of home. Clownish Ronald McDonald is as recognizable to the Happy Meal crowd as Santa Claus, and if you start with "two all-beef patties," most adults can finish the jingle.

The original Des Plaines restaurant is replicated as McDonald's #1 Store Museum, where visitors can see vintage equipment and an original manager's handbook with this early and politically incorrect directive: "Personnel with bad teeth, severe skin blemishes, or tattoos should not be stationed at service windows."

Admission is free. For museum hours and directions, visit www.mcdonalds.com/corp/about/museum_info.html.

McDonald's:

A worldwide fast-food chain born in Illinois and easily recognized by the Golden Arches.

illinois
...kryptonite is outlawed

Look . . . down by the Metropolis courthouse. It's a bird, it's a plane . . . no . . . it really is the world's most famous crime fighter: Superman.

In 1972 the state of Illinois passed a resolution that officially made Metropolis the adopted "Home of Superman." It makes sense: This 7,000-resident community along the Ohio River is the only Metropolis listed in the United States Postal Code Directory. Everyone knows that the superhero lives and works in Metropolis. That whole Smallville, Kansas, thing was just a temporary stop on the road to bigger places.

The original Superman was faster than a speeding bullet, more powerful than a locomotive, and able to leap tall buildings in a single bound. Metropolis presents few challenges, though. There are no tall buildings in this southern Illinois hamlet, and crime is almost nonexistent.

What the town does have is a 15-foot bronze statue of the "man of steel" in front of the courthouse on Superman Square. The hometown paper has obligingly changed its name to *The Metropolis Planet*. There are a couple of phone booths, but it's best not to try to change clothes in them. The city police force sports embroidered patches with an image of the town's adopted son on their uniforms, but capes and tights on citizens are generally frowned upon except during the second week in June.

That's when visitors fly into town for the Superman Celebration, which includes a mock bank robbery, costume contests, and strong-man competitions. On the square you'll also find the Super Museum, a larger-than-life collection of Superman memorabilia and a place to purchase Superman collectibles. Now that's truth, justice, and the American way. For more information, visit www.supermancelebration.net or www.metropolischamber.com.

Metropolis:

The town that gave Superman a home.

illinois

... water makes the state map

No body of water has created more legend and lore than the Mississippi. Mark Twain, himself a riverboat captain for a time, immortalized it in his classic river tales *Tom Sawyer* and *Huckleberry Finn*. "The Father of Waters," "Old Man River," "The Mighty Mississippi"—call it what whatever nickname you like, this is the largest river system in the United States.

Stretching from East Dubuque on the north to Cairo on the south, the Mississippi River defines the entire western edge of Illinois, flowing 518 miles before it leaves the state and continues to the Gulf of Mexico. It has the third largest watershed in the world, with a drainage basin covering more than 1,245,000 square miles, including all or parts of 31 states and two Canadian provinces.

Illinois is one of the few states whose boundaries are almost entirely formed by waterways. The buoyant waters of Lake Michigan lap at the northeastern portion of the state and the Ohio washes the eastern border, while the Illinois River slices through the state's interior. Together with the Mississippi, they form a transportation network that funnels 60 percent of the nation's grain and oilseed exports and gives American agriculture an edge over foreign competitors.

You can trace the Mississippi down western Illinois by driving the Great River Road, a

Mississippi River:

The largest river system in the United States and the defining border of western Illinois.

nationally designated byway that meanders through 18 counties and past 15 locks and dams. The road dallies in communities where you can bike or hike on trails close enough to the water's edge to hear conversations aboard passing barges. In Alton the National Great Rivers Museum traces the history of the locks and Mississippi River navigation. From outdoor viewing platforms, watch barges and other craft lock through Melvin Price Lock and Dam No. 26.

South of Cairo, at Fort Defiance State Park, you can see a rippling line where the broad, brown Mississippi merges with the blue waters of the Ohio River. Fort Defiance, a Civil War post commanded by General Ulysses S. Grant, guarded the confluence and became the supply base for the Union's western thrust into the Confederacy.

illinois
...finding a fungus is a spring ritual

Europe can have its truffles—Illinois has the morel. Each spring, as Mother Nature begins rousting herself from a long winter's nap, hunters start combing the woodlands in search of this ephemeral fungus.

The wild morel, a cranial-looking mushroom, can emerge in the southern regions of the state as early as late March. The season stretches into mid-May to the north. Veteran morel seekers know it's time when the willows and gooseberry bushes begin to show green and the oak leaves are the size of mouse ears.

Fanning out like prospectors, the hunters tiptoe through the woodlands on their quest. Some simply hunger for the morel's distinct nutty flavor, but most become infected with the fever of the find. Peering beneath elm trees and along old rail beds, they seek their quarry. Those who know where to look jealously protect their claims. Commercial morels can be found on the grocery shelf, but they are poor substitutes for the yeasty wild morsels that are the essence of earth itself.

Morels, which are native to every Midwestern state, resemble a conical sponge on a stalk and are typically 2 to 4 inches tall. When split, the body is hollow, with the base and the stem connected at the cap. Beware: There are false morels, which are inedible imposters.

Morel Mushrooms:

Small, edible, down-to-earth delights found in the woodlands during the early spring.

Illinois boasts one of the largest morel-mushroom-hunting contests in the nation. Each spring 650-plus morel maniacs take to the woods near the small town of Magnolia and compete for trophies for finding the most, the biggest, and the smallest mushrooms. For more information, visit the Events page at www.morelmania.com.

illinois
. . . landmarks get down and dirty

Since 1876 the eyes of Illinois farmers have focused on the ears rooted in the Morrow Plots, an unassuming one-tenth acre of Flanagan silt loam soil situated in the heart of the University of Illinois (U of I) campus.

When corn was first planted here—the site of the world's longest-term continuous corn plot and the United States' oldest agronomic experiment fields—Illinois farm wage rates were $15 a month, and corn sold for 30 cents a bushel. The state's average corn yield was 30 bushels an acre, about one-quarter of today's production, and two-thirds of the country's population lived on farms.

Inspired to conduct tests that would yield results "suggestive to these practical farmers," George E. Morrow, U of I's first dean of agriculture, and agriculture professor Manley Miles sowed the experimental seeds. Burning questions of the day begged answers: If corn were planted year after year on the same field, would yields decline? If so, how soon and how severely? Would rotating corn with other crops help maintain the soil's productivity?

Illinois farmers can tip their bill caps in appreciation for the knowledge harvested by Miles and Morrow, the site's namesake. A grateful nation also gave its nod, designating the Morrow Plots a National Historic Landmark in 1968. Today the area is distin-

guished as one of the few landmarks in the country to remain a working research site. Under constant study are the effects of fertilizers, crop rotation, climate, and drainage on total yields.

Folks at the U of I know good dirt when they see it, too. So hallowed is this plot that the neighboring undergraduate library, constructed in 1969 and situated due west, was built below ground so as not to cast a shadow on sun-loving shoots. Think twice before calling it "mud." Small vials of Morrow Plot soil, granted to select University donors, are akin to gold.

The site's true treasure was foretold by Andrew Sloan Draper, University of Illinois president from 1894 to 1904: "The wealth of Illinois is in her soil, and her strength lies in its intelligent development."

Morrow Plots:

The oldest corn test plots in the nation.

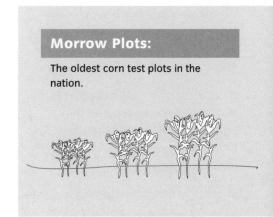

Think of the Morton Arboretum as a giant leaf collection. This 1,700-acre outdoor museum is filled with 3,700 different kinds of trees, shrubs, and plants from more than 60 countries. Grade-school students lucky enough to frequent the public garden have a major head start on homework when it comes time to gather specimens. (One warning: The caretakers frown on plucking, but you can get permission to pick up leaves that have fallen naturally.) The park is also a great place to find help when identification gets difficult.

Joy Morton, owner of the Morton Salt Company, started this horticultural haven in 1922. His father, Julius Sterling Morton, secretary of agriculture under President Grover Cleveland, was the originator of Arbor Day and adopted "Plant trees" as the family motto. The dutiful son embraced this creed and began transforming his estate in Lisle into the arboretum that bears his name today. In addition to amassing an amazing array of plants, the center does valuable research on how to keep them healthy.

Cars can roam the 9 miles of paved roads. Most visitors hop aboard the Acorn Express, an open-air tram that offers a one-hour guided tour. Hikers will find 14 miles of trails to explore.

See an art exhibit, take a yoga class, paint a picture, go birding, or just take a deep breath and relax. The children's garden is a magical place where kids age 2 to 10 can play and learn. "Live on the Hedge" is a one-acre maze that offers seven destinations, or plant rooms, where visitors will find interesting flowers, leaves, and bark. Tree climbing is not allowed, but a 12-foot-high lookout platform built around a 60-foot-tall sycamore tree is a fun place to watch family and friends navigate the maze.

Summers bring a season of theatre hikes (nonstrenuous walks culminating in outdoor drama performances) and twilight concerts. So pack a picnic or order one from the garden's Ginkgo Room and Restaurant, which overlooks the on-site lake. The Fall Color Festival runs every weekend during October, when the oaks, maples, and birches are in full color. For more information, visit www.mortonarb.org.

Morton Arboretum:

A research center and collection of woody plants in natural settings, open year-round.

illinois
...a hometown fills with sweethearts

Never mind the 800 miles that separate Atlantic City, New Jersey, and Hoopeston, Illinois. Winning a beauty pageant in this southeastern Illinois community is a major stepping-stone toward the Miss America title.

Since 1941 the friendly farming village of Hoopeston has been inviting runners-up from Miss America state preliminary competitions to compete for the title of Miss National Sweetheart. The pageant began as a way to attract more tourists to the town's annual Sweetcorn Festival. Not even the most optimistic planner could have predicted how the event would focus the national spotlight on this unlikely setting.

It's the ultimate in second chances. Many of the talented contestants subsequently win state titles, not to mention significant scholarship dollars. And since 1970 eight women who have won the National Sweetheart Pageant have gone on later to win Miss America.

The pageant is not officially affiliated with Miss America, but it uses some of the same judges and a similar point system. It's come to be considered a barometer for those who are serious about pageant competition. Some years a dozen or more contestants in an individual Miss America pageant will find they've also competed for the Sweetheart title.

National Sweetheart Pageant:

A nationwide annual beauty contest held in the town of Hoopeston that proves no one is ever second best.

As for the Sweetcorn Festival, it looks more like a county fair than a place for beauty contestants. Carnival rides, tractor pulls, and sweetcorn-eating are all part of the hometown festivities. The pageant is held in the local Civic Center, where spectators gather in everything from cocktail dresses to Levis.

Never heard of the title? Hoopeston spends little on publicity and makes few demands on winners, except to have them preside over the festival. It's not even a requirement that the winner like sweetcorn. But it helps.

illinois
. . . Mormonism inspires a city

To early Mormons the horseshoe bend of the Mississippi River—just east of where the Illinois, Iowa, and Missouri state borders meet—symbolized a turn toward tranquility.

Led by the group's founder, Joseph Smith, more than 5,000 Mormons fled religious persecution in northern Missouri and settled here in 1839. They dubbed their haven Nauvoo, or "beautiful" in Hebrew.

Nauvoo soon was among the nation's 10 largest cities and, in Illinois, was outranked only by Chicago. Its grandeur, however, was second to none. The magnificent temple of the Church of the Latter-Day Saints, situated sentrylike on bluffs, overlooked a city filled with exquisite homes and shops.

Nauvoo's rapid growth and opulence, combined with the Mormons' heavy political influence and Smith's candidacy for president of the United States, eventually aroused suspicion and hostility. One faction established a newspaper to oppose Smith and, when it was destroyed, blamed the Mormon leader. Smith and several church elders were arrested and jailed 20 miles south of Nauvoo. On June 27, 1844, a mob attacked the jail, assassinating Smith and his brother. Two years later, adversaries burned the temple.

Although most members fled Illinois and settled in Salt Lake City, Utah, Mormon

Nauvoo:

A western Illinois town that once was a haven for thousands of Mormons.

ideals never truly left the prairie. Resurrected in 2002 and again dominating the vista is the majestic Temple of Nauvoo. Built on its original site, the temple replicates Smith's original structure, right down to its gleaming limestone exterior and hand-crafted doors and window frames.

The temple also lies at the heart of a religious reclamation. Hundreds of Mormon missionaries regularly stay in settlement homes built by the church, and tourist buses from Salt Lake City arrive daily at the town's Joseph Smith Visitor's Center, located at 149 Water Street.

For more information, check out www.visit nauvoo.org or call (877) NAUVOO–1.

illinois
... piers have nine lives

Next time someone suggests you take a long walk on a short pier, head straight to the shores of Chicago's Lake Michigan, where you'll wander a wharf whose reincarnations rival those of the proverbial cat's nine lives.

Municipal Pier, as it was originally called, opened on June 25, 1916. The structure stretched 3,000 feet into the lake and measured 292 feet wide, monumental proportions reflective of Chicago's "enlightened city government." And although it earned its keep as a hardworking freight port, Municipal Pier gussied up, too, docking massive steamships and hosting extravagant exhibitions.

Next up, Uncle Sam. The military was in its genes from birth—the pier served as a recruiting and training site, detention camp, and carrier pigeon station—but it officially became Navy Pier in 1941, when the U.S. Navy christened the quay as a naval aviation training ground for mechanics. By 1946 a total of 60,000 sailors had "graduated" from the pier. Damaged planes often were unloaded there, and flyers trained on two converted paddlewheel steamers moored at the pier.

The 1950s saw the GI Bill and Navy Pier's leap into higher learning. A University of Illinois satellite until 1965, this was the only campus worldwide to boast classrooms that jutted more than a half mile into water.

The pier continued to host conventions and trade shows through the late 1960s before diving into disuse until 1975. It resurfaced in 1976, when the grand ballroom was renovated. Chicago Fest was held there from 1978 to 1982, and by 1989 the newly created Metropolitan Pier & Exposition Authority was fast-tracking plans for the pier's redesign.

Transfigured by a $277 million renovation, the pier made a full return to glory as a municipal monument on July 12, 1995. Among 50 acres of attractions are two anchored in the past: a musical merry-go-round with 36 custom-made menagerie animals and historic Navy Pier scenes on its carousel; and a 148-foot-high Ferris wheel, reminiscent of the structure that first whirled visitors to the 1893 Columbian Exposition.

Go ahead and take a long walk. First step: www.navypier.com.

Navy Pier:

A historic port located on the shore of Lake Michigan and revitalized as a commercial and entertainment hub.

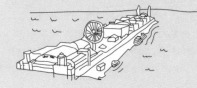

illinois
... freedom rings from New Philadelphia

Frank McWorter was ahead of his time. The former slave moved his family to Illinois in 1836 and started a town, the first in America legally founded by an African American.

New Philadelphia isn't even a ghost town today. All that's left of the original 42-acre settlement is a highway marker on a Pike County back road. Or is it?

In 2002 archaeologists began digging up answers about this unique community where blacks and whites once commingled, went to school together, and intermarried. Most archaeology studies of African Americans focus on pre-emancipation slave dwellings. New Philadelphia offers the chance to study what was an integrated population before and after the Civil War.

McWorter's story is worth telling. He had been a slave in Kentucky before he bought his freedom in 1819 at age 42 by mining and selling saltpeter. In 1831 this man, known as "Free Frank," acquired land in the sparsely populated area of western Illinois between the Illinois and Mississippi Rivers. Eventually he earned enough money from farming and selling land to buy 16 more family members out of slavery.

He had big dreams for his settlement. Main Street was 80 feet wide and broader than many New York City byways. McWorter had the town professionally surveyed, divided

into 44 lots, and registered with the state of Illinois. New Philadelphia's heyday came during the mid-1850s, though Free Frank died in 1854.

The town's demise began when the railroad bypassed it in 1869. By 1870 New Philadelphia was virtually dead, although a small white population occupied the area until 1940. Whether archaeology will be able to fully document racial harmony in this small place is not known. Satellite technology coupled with deed and census data is helping researchers locate house foundations and past domestic sites below the plow line.

The new dream is that New Philadelphia might one day become a state or national park. At the very least, the town's history is now being recorded as national history. That seems fitting since Free Frank McWorter was all about second chances.

New Philadelphia:

Town founded by a freed slave, and a rare example of integration in frontier America.

SITE of NEW PHILADELPHIA
SEPTEMBER 6, 1836

illinois

...getting grounded is a great time

It's not touted as a vacation spot, but perhaps world travelers should reconsider. Because here's a place where you can select from more than 100 restaurants and shops; visit a Kids on the Fly exhibit complete with an air traffic control tower and a cargo plane; gawk at a four-story Brachiosaurus dinosaur; gear up or down with a workout or massage; and ride for miles on a train—free. You can even go to church.

All while waiting to take off for your real destination.

Situated 17 miles from Chicago, O'Hare International enjoys the dubious distinction of being one of the world's two busiest airports in terms of passenger traffic. It usually cruises right below Hartsfield-Jackson Atlanta International.

With daily flights from O'Hare to more than 60 foreign and about 130 domestic destinations, chances are one's going your way. More than 190,000 passengers a day pass through this Chicago hub's four terminals, and most deem the experience—if not always the skies—friendly.

Constructed in 1942–43 as a manufacturing plant for Douglas C-54s during World War II, the Orchard Place Airport/Douglas Field, as it originally was known, also stored many rare or experimental planes, including captured enemy aircraft. When Douglas production moved to the West Coast in 1945,

O'Hare International Airport:

One of the world's two busiest airports, and headquarters for United Airlines.

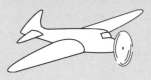

the City of Chicago expanded the site for future aviation needs and renamed it in honor of Chicago native Lt. Cmdr. Edward "Butch" O'Hare, a World War II flying ace and Congressional Medal of Honor recipient.

O'Hare's runways really earned their wings in the 1950s, when Midway Airport, previously Chicago's high flier, couldn't accommodate the first generation of jets. O'Hare was groomed as the city's main airport, and by the mid-1960s, more people passed through it annually than Ellis Island had processed in its entire existence.

"Passing through" remains O'Hare's biggest perk. And because not everyone appreciates the occasional grounding or delay, a $6 billion revamp of airport runways and a new terminal complex are under way, improvements projected to decrease "vacation time" by 79 percent.

illinois
. . . a ghost town attracts tourists

Broken shutters bang in the breeze. Tumbleweeds and an occasional stray dog skitter down a dusty boulevard. Shhh . . . is that calliope music wafting on the air?

Entering Old Shawneetown is like walking onto the set of a spaghetti western. This ghost town was once a bustling southern Illinois city and is still so filled with history that tourists come to marvel at the remains.

The Ohio River gave this town life and took it away. Named for the Indian tribe that once made the region home, Shawneetown was a famous gateway to the West for immigrants floating down the Ohio. Nearby salt springs initially attracted the interest of the federal government in the early 1800s. For more than a century, Shawneetown could boast that Washington, D.C., was the only other city in the nation established by an act of Congress.

Unfortunately, spring floods were an annual event. Record-high waters in 1937 finally convinced townspeople to move the town a few miles inland, reducing "Old" Shawneetown to a handful of hard-core residents.

Old Shawneetown:

A once-thriving gateway to the West, now a ghost town along the Ohio River.

The watermarks of this fatal flood can still be seen on the fine Doric columns of the Bank of Illinois at Shawneetown. This 1839 Greek Revival structure with an imposing flight of steps and sandstone portico is the town's enduring landmark and a reminder that Illinois banking began here. One local legend holds that Shawneetown's conservative bankers once refused a loan to Chicago, believing that a village so far from their end of the state would never amount to much. Historians doubt the story, and only ghosts are left to defend the tale.

illinois
... heavenly apparitions occur on the 13th

Every year millions of pilgrims visit Belleville's Our Lady of the Snows, the nation's largest outdoor Catholic shrine with 200 acres of chapels, prayer benches, grottos, and gardens. And of the faithful, one in particular—an elderly gentleman by the name of Ray Doiron—appears to know the shrine's namesake personally.

Doiron, who lives in southern Illinois near Belleville, claims that he has communed with the Virgin Mary every month on the 13th since January 1993. She appears to him as he prays the rosary at the shrine's Lourdes Grotto, her robes billowing and surrounded by bright light. Mary stays for about 45 minutes and always leaves Doiron with a message, typically "Pray, pray, pray," or "Beware of Satan always!"

Although most don't speak Mary's language, visitors still feel the vibes of this serene, spiritual place. Constructed in 1958 by the Missionary Oblates of Mary Immaculate on bluffs overlooking the Mississippi River valley, the shrine takes its name from the oldest Marian devotion in the Catholic Church, dating to A.D. 352. According to legend, on the night of August 4 a wealthy Roman couple prayed to Mary, asking her what to do with their riches when they died. The Virgin answered in their dreams. "Build a church," she said, promising to identify the location with a sign the next morning. At dawn Esquiline Hill was covered with newly fallen snow, despite Rome's extreme heat. St. Mary Major, the church constructed there, still stands.

Illinois' commemoration of this miracle debuted with two devotional sites, and today 12 areas span the landscape, including the Mary Chapel, Mother's Prayer Walk, and Agony Garden. Many Bible scenes are carved in marble, tiled in mosaic, or gilded in gold.

In 1998 an illuminated, 85-foot Millennium Spire was dedicated as a beacon of inspiration for a better world in the third millennium. Equally enlightening are the one million Christmas lights that lead auto-bound pilgrims on a journey toward a final Nativity scene. Plan your trip by visiting www.snows.org, and find out more about the monthly apparitions at www.apparitions.org/Doiron.html.

Our Lady of the Snows:

The largest outdoor Catholic shrine in America, where apparitions of the Virgin Mary are purported to occur.

illinois
... moldy medicine saves lives

Penicillin is serious medicine, but it has a corny connection to Illinois. Think back to grade-school history lessons, and you'll recall that London scientist Alexander Fleming wasn't very tidy. He waited so long to wash his bacteria-crusted lab dishes that they grew an icky, sticky, stinking mold. Then he noticed that disease-causing bacteria didn't grow where the mold had grown. He called his discovery "mold juice" and, later, penicillin. The British were able to convert penicillin to a stable powder, but they couldn't quite figure out how to mass-produce the drug.

In 1941 two British scientists came to Illinois armed with a small package of penicillin in brown powder form. Their mission was to work with the Americans to grow the drug in quantity and keep it out of the hands of the Nazis. Researchers at the United States Department of Agriculture lab in Peoria were already experimenting with growing molds in deep vats as part of a quest to find new uses for farm products.

One of the Peoria scientists, Andrew J. Moyer, found that steep water from wet corn milling (a process in which corn is soaked in a water solution to release its starch) made a nutritious medium for growing penicillin. He added milk sugar to the corn-water and was able to increase penicillin yields even more.

Moyer still wasn't satisfied, however, and started to search for a more productive strain of the mold. One man's trash is another's treasure. A fungus growing on a cantaloupe in a garbage can outside a Peoria fruit market was just what the doctor ordered. Soon the United States drug industry was using Moyer's new mold recipe to produce the miracle medicine in volume. Penicillin was available on June 6, 1944, to treat Allied troops wounded on D-Day, vanquishing the horrible infections that claimed soldiers in earlier wars.

In 1940 penicillin was priceless. In 1943 it cost $20 per dose and by 1946, only 55 cents per dose. Today it is one of the most inexpensive and widely used medicines in the world.

Penicillin:

Powerful antibiotic whose mass production was made possible by a Peoria scientist and the miracle crop of corn.

illinois

... birds become beasts

Bizarre beasts like Bigfoot can only dream of measuring up to Illinois' man-eating Piasa Bird. Just about everyone who lives in or around the city of Alton knows the story.

The fable goes back to 1673, when famous explorers Father Jacques Marquette and Louis Joliet floated down the Mississippi River and made a diary entry describing a huge, birdlike monster painted high on the bluffs. They called it Piasa (pronounced "PIE-a-saw") and deemed it to be "as large as a calf with horns like a deer, red eyes, a beard like a tiger's, a face like a man, the body covered with green, red and black scales, and a tail so long it passed around the body, over the head, and between the legs."

Several myths surround the creature. The oldest and most famous of these credits the Illini Indians with the name Piasa, meaning "bird that devours men" or "bird of the evil spirit." According to legend, whole villages were gobbled up before the Chief of the Illini, Ouatoga, successfully devised a plan to defeat the dragonlike demon with poisoned arrows. To honor Ouatoga's bravery, a picture of the fierce Piasa Bird was painted upon the bluff and an arrow shot in tribute each time the likeness was passed.

Piasa Bird:

A giant flying dragon painted on the bluffs along Illinois' Great River Road near Alton.

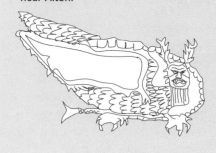

Over the years guns replaced arrows, and historians wrote of a painting etched into the cliffs worn away by "ten thousand bullet holes." Land developers eventually destroyed what was left of the painted bird, but the tale lived on. Today the Piasa Bird flies again in the form of a re-created 48-by-22-foot painting on the bluffs above Illinois' Great River Road, near the confluence of the Illinois and Mississippi Rivers.

illinois
. . . a pickup is more than just a line

It's no secret: America has an ongoing love affair with the pickup truck. Today's pickups are so cool, they're hot. It doesn't matter if you're 16 or 60; down-home or dressed up, the pickup has become something anyone can drive anywhere.

So while you're tooling around town in your Ford F-150 or pondering if you need a Dodge with Hemi under the hood, consider that all this truckin' got started in Illinois. The first pickup was a box on wheels called the King High-Wheeler. Built in 1896 by Chicago machinist A. W. King, the open-air contraption seated two people and hauled light cargo on what resembled a wagon with a flatbed rear deck. Dozens of other manufacturers quickly entered the marketplace.

These days the state is birthing what is being promoted as the biggest bad boy to come down the road. Enter the International CXT, a giant pickup that makes the Hummer look like a Matchbox toy. CXT is short for "commercial extreme truck," and it's one of the Godzilla-size pickups coming from International Truck and Engine in Warrenville. At just over 9 feet high, the 7300 CXT weighs about seven tons unloaded and gets 7 to 10 miles per gallon of diesel fuel.

Pickup Truck:

A workhorse vehicle for some and rugged personal transportation for others.

Of the 82.5 million private and commercial trucks registered in the United States, 3.3 million reside in Illinois, and 31 percent of those are pickups. According to the latest U.S. Census, Illinois has one pickup for every eight licensed drivers.

Doctors and lawyers are just as likely to be found driving trucks as farmers and ranchers. But manufacturers still use the pickup's work-ethic image to cultivate a macho appeal. A truck, it seems, is quintessential Americana—rugged, hard-working, and individualistic.

illinois

... bunnies aren't really rabbits

Chicago native and *Playboy* magazine founder Hugh Hefner chased bunches of bunnies in his day, but not the long-eared, hippity-hop, Peter Cottontail breed familiar to fellow Illinoisans.

Instead, the publications magnate pursued them as "playthings of the animal world." And in Hefner's universe these randy critters reproduced everywhere—as buxom, scantily clad, and spike-heeled female servers in his clubs nationwide; as his private jet, "Big Bunny," and its specially trained "Jet Bunnies," or flight attendants; and as the ubiquitous tuxedoed rabbit head logo, which marks all *Playboy* products and publications.

A University of Illinois alumnus, Hefner became a "magazine nut" in college, buying as many monthly periodicals as he could afford and starting a campus humor publication called *Shaft*. Despite a penchant for words, he opted for a psychology degree over journalism.

Hefner's concept for *Playboy* (nearly named *Stag Party*) was a breezy, sophisticated read for "city-bred" guys that combined "girlie" features (read: centerfold) with quality articles. In 1953—armed with minimal editorial experience, some buddies, $600 in loans, and about $8,000 raised from stock in HMH Publishing Co., Inc., sold to 40 acquaintances—he printed the first *Play-*

boy from his Windy City offices. At 50 cents a copy, the 53,991 issues sold exceeded even Hefner's wildest fantasies.

The first Chicago Playboy Club followed in 1960, and by 1967 Hefner had moved his offices to the former Palmolive Building, among the city's most prestigious and attractive structures.

Today nearly 10 million Americans—82 percent male, 18 percent female—peruse *Playboy* monthly, and 17 franchised editions are published overseas. Stories about the magazine's eccentric creator are equally prolific: extravagant A-list bashes at his 100-room Playboy Mansion; an immense circular, vibrating and rotating bed that often doubles as his office; and a 36-Pepsi-a-day habit.

This bunny tale's only casualties? Playboy Clubs, the last of which closed in 1986 due to "changing consumer trends."

Playboy Magazine:

Hugh Hefner's scantily clad, Chicago-based publication dynasty.

illinois
. . . spinach fuels an icon

He's an unlikely hero—a short, balding, ornery sailor with a long fuse and a keen sense of fair play. But everyone seems to identify when Popeye finally says, "Thas' all I can stands, 'cause I can't stands no more!"

We love him for his unpretentious "I yam what I yam." Not even Bugs Bunny has had such an impact on vegetable consumption. Forget steroids—everyone knows a can of spinach is all that's needed to develop a set of bulging forearms.

The cartoon character Popeye the Sailor may have been born in a typhoon off Santa Monica, California, but his creator, Elzie Crisler Segar, was a product of Chester, Illinois. Popeye, his pencil-thin love Olive Oyl, hamburger-eating Wimpy, and the rest of the gang were mostly based on real people from this southeastern Illinois village.

Segar decided to become a cartoonist at age 18 by taking a correspondence course. By 1919 and his 25th birthday, he'd made it to New York and was drawing a daily strip called *Thimble Theatre*. Olive Oyl, Castor Oyl, and Ham Gravy were his original cast. One day Castor Oyl needed a sailor to navigate his ship to Dice Island. The old salt he chose down by the docks was Popeye, who immediately stole the show.

A statue of Popeye can be found in Chester's riverfront park, and the Popeye Picnic held each September (www.popeye picnic.com) celebrates his ongoing popularity. Fans who stay "strong to the finich" will find the Popeye Museum and Spinach Can Collectibles store (www.popeyethesailor .com; 618–826–4567) in downtown Chester. Just don't be surprised if someone turns to you and says, "You'll eat yer spinach and likes it!"

Popeye:

America's favorite cartoon sailor, an invention of Illinois native Elzie Crisler Segar.

illinois
... the grass grows tall

Imagine the early explorers' astonishment when they came across a sea of grass. Thick growths of tall bluestem and other wild grasses stretched across the land that would become Illinois. Flowers of brilliant hues were scattered everywhere, with nary a tree or shrub in sight.

At first settlers were afraid to live among these uncultivated grasses, which towered so high that even a man on horseback was hard-pressed to see across the horizon. They adopted the French word *prairie,* meaning "meadow," to describe the plains that were so unlike their forested European homelands. And pioneers often called their wagons prairie schooners, invoking an analogy to sailing vessels upon the sea.

The state's landscape was forever changed when prairie soils were discovered to be more fertile than forest soils. Plowing the prairie turned up some of the most productive topsoil in the world, but it took a toll on what made it special.

"The Prairie State" is still a common nickname for Illinois, despite the fact that very little prairie is left. Twenty-two million acres (more than 60 percent of Illinois land) were covered in shimmering grasses prior to settlement; only 2,300 acres of the state's rich natural heritage remain.

Prairie State:

An Illinois nickname that recalls the millions of acres of grassland found by early explorers.

You can see what the region once looked like by visiting one of the parks where big bluestem grass, blazing star, prairie dock, and other native plants are being reestablished. One of the larger remnants grows south of Chicago at Goose Lake Prairie State Natural Area.

Big bluestem was named Illinois' official prairie grass in 1989. This dominant plant of the tallgrass prairie is also called "turkey foot" grass because its three-pronged seed head resembles a bird's foot.

illinois

...you can grow up to be president

Commanders-in-chief pull no particular rank when it comes to birthplaces, which may explain why only President Ronald Reagan claimed native Illinois status.

The northwest town of Tampico, population 735, welcomed our 39th president to his first home, a second-floor apartment situated over a downtown bakery, on February 6, 1911. As a boy Reagan lived mere miles away in Dixon, where he honed his acting skills on the Northside High School stages. Reagan next worked his way through nearby Eureka College, balancing economics and sociology with a spot on the football team. Today the Reagan Trail guides visitors through the trio of towns. Along the marked route you can visit Reagan's homes and sample his family's favorite recipes at the Dutch Diner in downtown Tampico.

In its benevolence, the state also adopted two homeboy wannabes: Ulysses S. Grant and Abraham Lincoln, favorite sons of Galena and Springfield, respectively.

Civil War general and hero Ulysses S. Grant was also Galena's champion. In 1860 a financially strapped Grant moved his family to this northwestern Illinois River town (home to Grant's parents) so he could work in his father's leather shop. But when the Civil War started in 1861, Grant left this "uncongenial" position and enlisted, ultimately engineering key Union victories such as the Battle of Vicksburg. Townsfolk

Presents:

Commanders-in-chief native to, and adopted by, Illinois.

welcomed Grant back with open arms on August 18, 1865, and gave him a handsome, Italianate house overlooking the river. Extensively renovated in 1955, the Grant home offers visitors the same view enjoyed by the 18th president, who served from 1869 to 1877.

The Central Illinois communities of New Salem and Springfield shared 23 years of Abraham Lincoln's life, and dozens of regional sites richly reflect "Honest Abe" as husband, father, attorney, and legislator. Leaving his beloved Springfield for Washington, D.C., as president-elect in 1861, the nation's 16th president said, "No one, in my situation, can appreciate my feelings of sadness at this parting."

illinois
. . . kids ditch school for Casimir

Illinois kids are crazy about Casimir Pulaski. That's because every year on the first Monday of March, school lets out to honor this man. Never mind that he never set foot in Illinois, or anyplace else in the American Midwest. Small wonder that parents, who almost always must be reminded of the state holiday each year, invariably respond, "Casimir who?"

Casimir Pulaski, better known as Kazimierz Pulaski in his home country of Poland, fought to defend his nation against Russian forces in the 1760s and 1770s. When those efforts failed to prevent the partition of Poland, Pulaski fled and was recruited by Benjamin Franklin to fight for American independence from the British.

Pulaski's efforts during the Revolutionary War must have been monumental, because there are statues of him in several states. Illinois named a county, town, and various streets after the fellow, but so far it is the only state to officially observe his contributions with a state holiday. The day off was sanctioned by the Illinois General Assembly in 1977, which explains why a few generations of folks missed the history lesson and now question the need for an official vacation day.

Illinois is home to nearly one-tenth of the Polish-American population, which partially explains the connection. But just a wee minute . . . the Irish were one of the largest immigrant groups to settle in the United States, and they have a very large and influential group in Chicago. Shouldn't school be dismissed on March 17, too?

No such luck, kids. You'll have to settle for taking in Chicago's massive annual St. Patrick's Day Parade (always held on Saturday) and celebrating as the Chicago River is dyed a rich, emerald hue.

Pulaski Day:

An Illinois state holiday mostly celebrated by children who escape a day of school.

illinois

... getting squashed is a tasty alternative

Glance out the car window as you cruise Interstate 74 east or west past Morton, and you'll see vast fields filled with rows of plants bearing pale-orange oblong gourds. Exit the interstate, and you'll arrive at the crop's final destination: the Nestlé/Libby's processing plant, the world's largest pumpkin cannery. Up to 150,000 tons of Dickenson squash—as these watermelon-shaped oddities are officially classified—are processed here annually. That's the equivalent of 90 million pumpkin pies.

Eighty percent of the nation's pumpkin population comes from within a 90-mile radius of Morton, population 14,000. That makes Illinois the top pumpkin producer and processor in the United States. Financially speaking, each 20-pounder fetches a pretty price for a somewhat lumpy mass of thick rind, dry flesh, and spittin' seeds. Nearly 12,300 orange acres are harvested in the state each year, with the total crop value exceeding $10 million.

In Morton, which was declared "Pumpkin Capital of the World" by a gubernatorial decree in 1978, thousands celebrate the beginning of canning season every September at the Pumpkin Festival. And thanks to the event's Punkin Chuckin' competition, Mortonites claim bragging rights for the world's longest pumpkin-chuck. The hurl

happened in 1998, when the Aludium Q-36 Pumpkin Modulator, a homemade contraption akin to a giant pea shooter, expelled a pumpkin from an 80-foot tube connected to an 1,800-gallon compressed air tank. Traveling at nearly the speed of sound, the 10-pound squash followed a graceful arc toward the horizon, only to land with a decidedly undignified "splat" 4,491 feet— nearly ½ mile—away.

See it all for yourself, and enjoy a big slice of homemade pumpkin pie while you're there. For more information, visit www.PumpkinCapital.com.

Pumpkins:

Members of the squash family, used for both pies and chuckin'.

illinois
... mosquitoes are a meal

Other bird-brained schemes are no match for the one hatched in Griggsville. Venture into this small west-central Illinois burg, and you'll find a large number of tall poles supporting birdhouses. Near the center of town, a 562-apartment avian high-rise juts above the skyline.

These are not just any ordinary birdhouses. They are purple martin homes. Purple martins, it seems, are very picky about their accommodations. In fact, the bluish-black bird got so finicky about where it hangs out that it once became endangered.

Around the same time, the people of Griggsville had their own problems. Clouds of blood-sucking mosquitoes were making summers insufferable, thanks to the proximity of the Mississippi and Illinois Rivers. The local Jaycees got irritated about the bug bites and started considering insect abatement, but they disliked the idea of pouring on pesticides.

Enter J. L. Wade, a nature lover, antenna manufacturer, and respected townsman who had studied up on a beneficial type of swallow called the purple martin. A single purple martin, he opined, could eat 2,000 mosquitoes per day. Wade was convinced that for a city-wide project to work, it would take a special house that would attract purple martins and keep out less savory species. An ornithologist was consulted

Purple Martin:

Type of swallow that dines on flying insects and gets preferential housing in Griggsville.

and a house designed, which Wade put his factory to work building.

Some 40 years later, Wade's company, now known as Nature House, Inc., continues to tweak the bird condo concept. Griggsville claims to be the Purple Martin Capital of the United States. Tourists buy T-shirts celebrating "America's most wanted bird."

The purple martin's consumptive capacity and unique preference for mosquitoes has never been proven. But bird populations have rebounded. Like the miracle of the swallows of Capistrano, the purple martins send scouts each spring to make sure their houses are in order before the rest of the martin colony migrates. That should be warning enough to mosquitoes to skedaddle.

illinois
. . . mop-topped duos doll up a town

Bright red smiles and triangular noses light every corner of the world's only officially licensed Raggedy Ann and Andy Museum, home to the original icons themselves. Clad in their trademark red, white, and blue outfits, with strings of crimson yarn hair, these beloved dolls have returned to their roots, lodging in the birthplace of their creator, artist Johnny Gruelle.

Born on December 24, 1880, in the small central Illinois town of Arcola, Gruelle grew up surrounded by the arts, literature, and music. And although he carved a successful career crafting illustrations for magazines and newspapers—including *Life, Cosmopolitan,* and *Good Housekeeping*—it was his humble pair of floppy rag dolls that captured the hearts of millions.

Gruelle's daughter likely was the muse for Raggedy Ann. Marcella suffered from a heart condition, and throughout her long illness her father, the "Raggedy Ann Man," spent many hours entertaining her with stories and plays starring one of her dolls. After Marcella died at age 13, Gruelle personified his memories in the form of little folks who would never lose their grins: Raggedy Ann and Andy, patented and trademarked in 1915 and 1918, respectively. By 1922 Gruelle's serialized "Adventures of Raggedy Ann and Andy" stories premiered in newspapers nationwide and, until his death in 1938, he wrote and illustrated at least one book a year.

Today children of all ages embrace this whimsical world. Gruelle's granddaughter, Joni Gruelle Wannamaker, welcomes thousands of museum visitors annually and cheerfully autographs dolls owned by 9- and 90-year-olds alike. Arcola residents play dress-up, too, donning pantaloons, jackets, breeches, and striped leggings for the Raggedy Ann and Andy parade, part of the annual May Festival.

The town spirit models make-believe at its best, says Wannamaker. "Everyone, it seems, has a Raggedy Ann or Andy story. They're the All-American dolls—always smiling, always floppy, always ready for a hug."

Raggedy lovers are welcome anytime at the museum's official Web site: www.raggedy ann-museum.org.

Raggedy Ann and Andy:

Rag doll duo created by Arcola native Johnny Gruelle and inducted into the National Toy Hall of Fame in 2002.

illinois

... you still get your kicks on Route 66

The classic scene remains etched in collective memory: A 1952 blue Chevy chugs along Illinois Route 66, its passengers peering from every window. Dad watches for a "gas for less" Sinclair station—should be ahead in Odell—while Mom looks for a lunch spot, maybe the Polka-Dot Drive In at Braidwood. The kids crane their necks for the next Burma Shave billboard's sing-song slogan: "If you don't know whose signs these are, you can't have driven very far—Burma Shave."

Signs, stations, diners, dives: Route 66 spawned them all. Created to link small towns with a national roadway, the two-lane road was named in 1926. By the time it was "continuously paved" in 1938, Route 66 traversed Main Street America—2,400 miles, three time zones, and eight states—from its origin at the corner of Jackson and Lakeshore Drives in Chicago to Los Angeles, California.

Every turn promised places to "get your kicks," and cross-country drivers took to the road in droves. Before too many miles, Route 66 was cemented in American culture, fueled by *Grapes of Wrath* author John Steinbeck, who christened it the "Mother Road." Songs and even a 1960s television series spread its fame farther still.

Illinois was the first state to boast that its portion was "slab all the way." From the Windy City south to Granite City, the 300-

> ### Route 66:
>
> America's "Mother Road" started in Chicago and stretched through the heart of Illinois.

plus miles of famed pavement are still practically bumper-to-bumper with members of "Mother's" eclectic brood: Springfield's Cozy Dog Drive-In, birthplace of the corn dog; Broadwell's Pig Hip Restaurant, named for its pork specialties; and Mount Olive's Soulsby Station, where "Fill 'er up" has echoed since 1926.

By 1977, however, these wide spots in the road could be bypassed via Interstate 55, and in 1985 the government officially canceled Route 66's designation.

A path less traveled? Not really. Rather than a conduit to all points west, today's historic Route 66 gets its kicks hosting kitschy retro getaways for nostalgic navigators. If you're one of the many throwbacks, start your journey with a visit to www.illinoisroute66 .com.

illinois
. . . the house is in the mail

The homes arrived by rail in boxcars filled with precut lumber and wooden kegs of nails. The kit contained everything from the paint and plaster to the kitchen sink. Sears, Roebuck and Company even sent two small trees for planting in the front yard.

From 1908 to 1940 more than 100,000 American families purchased homes from the same catalog that sold boots and bathing suits. Nowhere did these houses influence the landscape more than in Illinois.

The largest remaining collection of Sears mail-order homes still stands in Carlinville. In 1918 the Standard Oil Company purchased 156 Sears homes to house their coal miners in this community southwest of Springfield. Almost 90 years later, all but four of the homes still stand. The Chicago-area community of Downers Grove also claims more than 80 of the homes, and both communities offer periodic historic tours of the houses.

Sears was not the only company in the mail-order business, but it was the largest. Customers could chose from 450 different models with many variations and custom design options. The kits averaged about 30,000 numbered wood pieces that were assembled according to a plan book, like a giant model.

Sears Home:

A house ordered by mail from the Sears, Roebuck catalog.

The mail-order houses delivered new concepts such as drywall and asphalt shingles. Modern homebuyers were introduced to central heating, indoor plumbing, and electricity. Not only could the buyer order the entire house and furnishings from Sears, but the company would also finance the purchase with a home mortgage.

Liberal loan policies and the Depression combined to kill the service. But the mail-order homes are treasured windows to the past. For more information, visit www.searshomes.org.

illinois
... everybody laughs last

In 1951 reporter A. J. Liebling wrote a derisive article about Chicago in the *New Yorker* magazine, dubbing it "The Second City"—a sad, New York City wannabe.

But rather than get their Midwestern noses out of joint, a group of witty, creative, and intellectual University of Chicago students embraced the insult and wound up laughing all the way to the bank.

The Second City theater (SC), a Chicago landmark and national treasure, opened December 16, 1959, on North Wells Street. And while a face might launch a thousand ships, only The Second City can claim the launch of a thousand—give or take—multi-million-dollar comedy careers. Famous laughingstocks include John Belushi, Mike Myers, Bill Murray, Bonnie Hunt, Chris Farley, Harold Ramis, George Wendt, Shelley Long, Betty Thomas, Jim Belushi, Dan Aykroyd, Alan Arkin, and Joan Rivers.

From the start this City knew no limits. Shows were smart, original, and guaranteed to push the envelope. Improvisational workshops meant anything went (and everything did), and the 1960s climate was ripe for SC's brand of social and political satire. By the mid-1970s SC's popularity had spawned another groundbreaker, *Saturday Night Live,* which featured several notable graduates. Two of the more infamous—Dan Aykroyd and John Belushi—

also donned black coats, ties, hats, shoes, and sunglasses to bring their alter egos, Jake and Elwood, to the big screen in *The Blues Brothers*.

Today Second City "suburbs" include two resident stages and a training center—Donny's Skybox—that features student productions and alternative shows and teaches the art of improvisation and acting. Touring troupes take SC shows on the road and overseas.

Grab a seat for any Second City performance, and you'll see why Illinois takes its comedy seriously. For upcoming shows and schedules, visit www.secondcity.com.

The Second City:

Innovative, edgy Chicago-based comedy theater that launched the careers of famed funny people John Belushi, Dan Aykroyd, and Bill Murray.

illinois

... schools of sea creatures play show-and-tell

Sea dragons and stingrays and sharks. Oh, my! Piranhas and penguins and pipefish. Oh, my!

Exclamations of this sort float from every corner of Chicago's Shedd Aquarium, where two-million-plus visitors a year wander through a world swimming with more than 6,000 fish, reptiles, amphibians, mammals, and invertebrates representing about 750 different species.

Surrounded on three sides by its freshwater source—Lake Michigan—the aquarium's classical Greek-inspired Beaux Arts structure can be seen for miles. But the true wonders wriggle within Shedd's 200-plus tanks, which fill six galleries and exhibit halls. Press up to the glass and greet a Pacific white-sided dolphin, face-to-fin. Or wander an Amazon rain forest and make the acquaintance of anacondas and arawanas, fish that can leap about 3 feet from the water to snap insects, spiders—or maybe your nose.

Benefactor John Graves Shedd gave $2 million to build the facility, the world's largest when it opened in 1929. The aquarium's first residents arrived via a custom-built railroad car converted to a virtual traveling aquarium. Today most are "hooked" by the Aquarium's research vessel, which navigates worldwide. Species then travel to Chicago by air in oxygen-filled plastic bags packed in Styrofoam boxes.

Once newcomers reach their destination, habitats are meticulously re-created. The Oceanarium exhibit, for example, required 364 tons of salt for three million gallons of salt water—all mixed by aquarium staff. Every exhibit follows Shedd's dual mandate: show and tell, with an emphasis on protection and conservation.

Before you dive into Shedd's underwater world, take a quick look upward at recent renovations. A massive skylight, painted over for decades, now brightens the aquarium. And after sitting idle for 15 years, the aquatic animals that pose as numbers on the old, ornate rotunda clock once again tell time.

For more information, surf over to www.sheddaquarium.org.

Shedd Aquarium:

One of the oldest public aquariums in the world, situated on a peninsula jutting into Chicago's Lake Michigan.

illinois
. . . buildings go sky-high

It's easy to be on top of the world in Chicago. Just take the elevator to the Sears Tower Skydeck (www.theskydeck.com). On a clear day you can see for 50 miles and view four states—Illinois, Indiana, Michigan, and Wisconsin.

Whether the Sears Tower is actually the world's tallest building is up for debate. It stands 1,450 feet tall, but the rooftop antennas bring the total height to 1,730 feet. Folks in Taiwan figure they have the biggest bragging rights since a building in Taipei comes in at 1,670 feet without any doodads. But Taipei 101 has (as the name suggests) 101 stories, compared to 110 stories in the Sears Tower. The Petronas Towers in Kuala Lumpur also stake a claim in this game of one-upmanship; they measure 1,483 feet each but have only 88 floors.

Chicago's giant building, which opened in 1973, took three years and more than $150 million to build. To construct it architects combined several vertical skeleton sections or tubes—like a giant Erector Set—into one structure. Nine aligned tubes reach to different heights and give the building an interesting staggered appearance. The Skydeck is on the 103rd floor, and each year 1.5 million visitors bravely enter the elevators that hurtle upward at superhero-worthy speeds of 1,600 feet per minute.

Out on the rural Illinois prairie, another type of high-rise punctuates the horizon. Just as

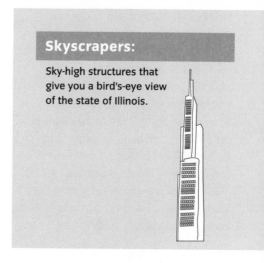

Skyscrapers:

Sky-high structures that give you a bird's-eye view of the state of Illinois.

a lighthouse serves as a beacon in a storm, the local grain elevator is often the point of reference for back-road travelers. Spotting one in the distance announces you've arrived, even if you're not sure where.

Each fall these granaries open their gates to accept a sea of grains and oilseeds from surrounding farms. Technology, transportation, and consolidation have shuttered many of the old-time wooden country elevators. Giant concrete silos and what look like the equivalent of monstrous corrugated tin cans now hold the grains that eventually help feed the world. But you can get a glimpse of the past at the J. H. Hawes Grain Elevator Museum in Atlanta. For more information, visit www.haweselevator.org.

illinois

. . . snakes have the right-of-way

Snakes alive! Twice a year Forest Service Road 345 in Illinois' Shawnee National Forest closes to allow thousands of snakes, toads, lizards, frogs, turtles, and other creepy-crawlies to wriggle to safety. Nature lovers gather each spring to watch as the snakes leave the warmth of their dens in the 350-foot-high bluffs to slither to the cooling lowland swamps. Come fall, the critters reverse direction and head back to hibernate for the winter in the rocky crevasses. Think of it as the herpetological equivalent of heading south for the winter.

So why do they cross the road? Easy: The 2.6-mile passage stretches squarely between the two migrating destinations. Locals once found sport in driving over the serpents, so in 1972 the Forest Service began giving right-of-way to the victims. Road 345 is the only government byway known to close for this reason. More than half the species of reptiles and amphibians known to inhabit Illinois have been spotted in this biologically diverse region, officially known as the LaRue Pine Hills Research Natural Area.

A walk down "Snake Road" isn't exactly like a slithery scene in an Indiana Jones movie. But tread carefully. Poisonous copperheads and western cottonmouths hang out with harmless five-lined skinks, northern fence

Snake Migration:

Mass movement of reptiles and amphibians that prompts the closure of Forest Service Road 345 in Shawnee National Forest.

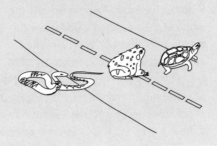

lizards, red-eared turtles, chorus frogs, and Ozark red-back salamanders. Ground temperatures dictate movement, but the road officially closes from March 15 to May 15 and again from September 1 to October 31.

Find the entrance to the natural area along Illinois State Route 3 about 30 miles north of Cairo, on the western edge of the Shawnee National Forest.

illinois
...beans are still magic

You won't find enormous beanstalks sprouting from the prairie, but even Jack and the Giant would agree that the million-plus acres of soybeans that grow here could easily trade for bags of gold.

Tiny in size but mighty in heart, these plain little pods pack the amazing ability to appear in everything from animal feed to pasta, paint, and pesticide—metamorphoses that earn the soybean the lofty title of "magic bean."

The charisma characterizes communities as well, most notably the central Illinois city of Decatur, known as the Soybean Capital of the World. Agribusiness giant Archer Daniels Midland (ADM), one of the world's top three soybean crushers, planted its global headquarters here, and soybean trade worldwide is based on prices FOB (free on board) in Decatur. Cruise the city and you'll spot banks; motels; electrical, towing, and cleansing-product companies; and even a radio station all named for the benevolent bean.

Soy is in the air, too. When the wind hails from the right direction, *l'aire du soybean* envelopes Decatur, wafting from ADM's processing facilities. The sharp scent is distinctive, and its "beauty" definitely lies in the nose of the sniffer. Some residents inhale with appreciation, while others wrinkle their nostrils in distaste.

Imported from China, soybeans first spouted on U.S. soil in the early 20th century; decades later, advanced processing techniques tap every part of this amazing commodity. Its range of commercial uses tops 350, and counting.

When Mom says, "Eat your soybeans," take heed. They're your single highest natural source of dietary fiber and provide eight essential amino acids not produced naturally by your body. This perk also may explain the soybean's most recent brave new frontier: Soy 7 pastas, produced by ADM, are casting lunch-hour spells in central Illinois' grade-school cafeterias.

Soybeans:

Oilseeds transplanted from China that now consume half of Illinois' agricultural acres and appear in hundreds of products.

illinois
. . . rocks are ravenous

Every year thousands of tourists ascend 140 feet to the top of Starved Rock—an enormous sandstone butte soaring from the Illinois River between LaSalle and Ottawa in northern Illinois.

The gargantuan granite takes its name from an infamous 1760s massacre. Seeking refuge from warring Potawatomi and Fox tribes, Illiniwek Indians climbed to the rock's summit, where instead of a haven, they found a hell. Enemies surrounded the base, cutting ropes or shattering buckets when the Illiniwek tried to get water and showering deserters with arrows as they descended. Trapped at the top, remaining tribe members chose to stand their ground and starve rather than face capture.

Brigands and outlaws are said to have had better luck years later, successfully finding sanctuary in the cliff's nearby canyons and caves.

Among the first to document the legendary site were Father Marquette and Louis Joliet, in 1673. Originally searching for a shorter route to China, the pair got as far as the Arkansas River before deciding to turn back and follow a shortcut to the Great Lakes, via the Illinois River. Fort St. Louis was constructed atop the peak in 1682, a bold statement by French explorers meant to make the English think twice about interfering with King Louis XIV's claim to the New World.

Starved Rock and the surrounding area became an Illinois state park in 1911. Today 15 miles of hiking and biking trails and 2,630 acres of thick forests—plus cabins, a lodge, and sparkling waterfalls—span this scenic region. The park's 18 canyons provide a type of time-travel experience, as clues from their sandstone walls indicate that they look much as they did 4,000 years ago.

A friendlier band now encircles the park's namesake. An intricate wooden platform, built around its circumference in 1981, protects the landmark from erosion caused by enthusiastic climbers.

Starved Rock:

A state park named for the legendary cliff where members of the Illiniwek tribe were massacred or starved to death.

illinois
... Satan's in the soda

Back in the late 1800s, folks likely thought twice before they visited Evanston on a Sunday.

Dubbed "Heavenston" for its Methodist-minded religious zeal, the town's Sabbath sin list stretched longer than a preacher's sermon: Thou shalt not read (unless it was the Bible). Thou shalt not swing (contraptions were chained up to quell temptation). Thou shalt not imbibe (unless you headed up the road to Chicago).

And, above all, thou shalt not slurp ice cream sodas. Loaded with sugar and bubbling like cauldrons, these hedonistic "intoxicants" were said to bring out the devil in unsuspecting souls.

As the story goes, this particular edict hit Mr. William Garwood, owner of Garwood's Drugstore, right in the sweet spot. There could be no day of rest for the wicked, he insisted, as sales of the enormously popular ice cream sodas supported his entire enterprise.

Garwood, already considered a bit avant-garde for rigging an electric bell to a tree in front of his drugstore and delivering orders "buggy-side," set out to skirt this sticky situation. He created a soda-less concoction—ice cream topped with a customer's choice of syrup. No bubbles, no temptation, no sin.

Sundaes:

Ice-cream-and-syrup treats created by Evanston entrepreneur William Garwood in response to an 1890s law prohibiting the sale of ice cream sodas on Sunday.

Originally called the "Sunday" soda, the spelling soon changed to "sundae" in deference to the Sabbath. And, to Garwood's delight, orders for sundaes started spilling over to Monday, Tuesday, Wednesday, and beyond. Ice cream sodas had met their match, and then some.

Garwood sold the drugstore years later, and it eventually was razed for a bank building. But residents still claim the sundae as their own, and the Evanston Historical Society obliges by hosting an annual ice cream social in September, a nod to the druggist's ingenuity.

And should you spend a Sunday here, you now have the town's blessing to visit a playground, read the newspaper, or even swig a soda.

illinois
...loudmouths dominate daytime TV

Boob-tube research reveals that the average couch potato would rather tune in to loudmouth Midwesterners than to verbose East- or West-coasters. And when you're talking long-windedness, Chicago—home to the modern American talk show—really cranks the volume.

The phenomenon started in 1974, when Phil Donohue launched his national show from the Windy City. Donohue's ratings rose as topics got bolder and he and his audience got louder, a no-fail talk-show formula. Next came Oprah Winfrey, fresh from Baltimore. Within one year of its September 8, 1986, debut, the *Oprah Winfrey Show* was number one among nationally syndicated talk shows.

Cameras soon rolled on scandals, makeovers, true confessions, and courtroom dramas, in the forms of the *Jerry Springer Show, Jenny Jones,* and *Judge Mathis,* a "real judge delivering real justice." And while celebrity hosts and guests snag the limelight, live audiences relish their five minutes of fame as well. Sure, studio prompts may tell you when to laugh or applaud. But land on the *Oprah Winfrey Show,* and you might win a new car or be invited to join Oprah's Book Club. Did your husband leave you for your younger sister? Sounds like next week's *Jerry Springer* episode.

Talk Show:

Top-rated Chicago-born television format, heavy on audience participation and host-celebrity-audience interaction.

Ironically, the nation's big-mouth bastion claims a quiet start to talk-show fame. Long before Hollywood lured the stars, Chicago was home to several movie studios, the largest of which was Essanay. In business from 1907 to 1917, Essanay launched the careers of early silent movie legends, including Charlie Chaplin, Gloria Swanson, and Ben Turpin.

Want to open your big mouth? Oprah Winfrey (www.oprah.com), Jerry Springer (312–321–5365), and Judge Mathis (1–888–VERDICT) are all ears.

illinois
... horses really can fly

They are Pegasus without wings, yet still able to fly. Ridden by Prince Charming, protected by empires, coveted by kings—the magnificent Lipizzan horses are more than a fairy tale, thanks to Illinois' Tempel Farms. Just north of Chicago at Wadsworth, the largest privately owned herd in the world performs the equivalent of equine ballet for adoring audiences.

Lipizzans are Europe's oldest domesticated breed of horse and represent 425 years of matching superior horses from across the globe. Despite their beauty, nobility, and rare combination of courage, strength, ability, and temperament, only 200 of the animals existed at the end of World War II. (Throughout history, war and lack of suitable food and shelter threatened the breed's existence.)

A Walt Disney movie, *The Miracle of the White Stallions,* tells the story of the daring rescue of the Lipizzans under orders of General George S. Patton. In 1958 steel millionaire Tempel Smith and his wife, Esther, began their own tactical revival of the breed by importing animals from Austria and breeding the Lipizzans in Illinois.

Tempel Farms opened its gates to the public in 1982 so the horses could show off their training in classical dressage. Crowds clamor as the elegant white stallions literally dance across the arena by leaping in

unison or hopping while reared on their back legs. These abilities come naturally to a Lipizzan, but they require unique communication between the horse and handler.

Once a rare and nearly endangered species, Lipizzans are now used by the Marine Corps color guard. President Reagan rode one, and there are an estimated 800 head in the United States and 3,000 head worldwide. For more information on performances and farm tours, visit www.tempelfarms.com.

Tempel Lipizzans:

Show-stopping horses that are trained and perform at Tempel Farms in Wadsworth.

illinois
... bicyclists brake for donuts

Talk about carb-counting. Even Lance Armstrong's eyes would glaze over on this calorie-filled cycling adventure. Tour de Donut was launched in 1988 as a spoof on the Tour de France and is held the second Saturday in July, in Staunton, to coincide with the world's premier bicycle race.

It is an eating exercise that would make donut-craving Homer Simpson giddy. Participants are given a five-minute deduction from accumulated racing time for each donut consumed. Yes, gluttons for punishment can eat enough to realize negative numbers. And no, that doesn't mean you finish before you start.

Spectators line the streets of this rural town just north of St. Louis to cheer as 500 riders make a beeline through the village and out into the countryside, where pastries await. The 30-mile course is interrupted with two eating stations spaced at 10-mile intervals.

Riders pedal furiously to the stops, then jump from their bikes and wolf down as many glazed donuts as they can stomach. The hundred-plus dozens consumed each year are served up by Jubelt's Bakery, a local shop that produces a thick, yeasty product that makes Krispy Kreme donuts look dinky.

Strategy abounds. Some cyclists smash stacks of donuts into thinner, supposedly more consumable globs of dough. Others eat them one by one. Some prefer to ride fast and eat less. Others simply pig out and take their own sweet time.

Prizes are given for the fastest time, the fastest time adjusted for donut consumption, and the most donuts consumed. Count on eating close to two dozen donuts and finishing the route in two hours or less if you want to be a competitive holey roller. For more information, visit www.bebike club.com.

Tour de Donut:

A zany bicycle race that rewards riders for eating donuts while going the distance.

illinois
...paths are paved with sorrow

About 11,500 years ago Indian tribes settled in the area now known as Shawnee National Forest, an idyllic stretch of land near the state's southern tip that brimmed with abundant wildlife, lakes, streams, and rivers.

But written within these 300,000 bountiful acres is another Native American story, one told through the thousands of tired and battered feet that tread the "Trail of Tears," or "Trail Where They Cried."

Between 1830 and 1850 an estimated 100,000 Choctaws, Chickasaws, Creeks, Cherokees, and Seminoles were forced from their homelands in the southeastern United States to Oklahoma as part of the Indian Removal Act of 1830. Huddled in blankets, they walked or traveled by horseback or wagon 800 miles. By the end of the mandatory exile, nearly 90,000 persons had been relocated. Approximately 8,000 had died.

Among the very last to leave their native homes were the Cherokees, who trekked the Trail of Tears during a massive migration in the fall and winter of 1838–39. Illinois represented the harshest part of their journey. Trudging through Golconda and across the state's southern edge, nearly 2,000 tribe members succumbed to illness, ill treatment, exhaustion, and exposure while waiting to cross the ice-choked Mississippi.

Trail of Tears:

The path in southern Illinois on which nearly 2,000 Cherokee died in the fall and winter of 1838–39.

Today, as in centuries past, thousands of visitors savor the natural beauty of Shawnee National Forest and the seven designated wilderness areas within: Bald Knob, Bay Creek, Burden Falls, Clear Springs, Garden of the Gods, Lusk Creek, and Panther Den. Most acknowledge the heartbreak witnessed by these hills as well, opting to walk a section of the path that represents one of our nation's most culturally devastating eras.

Descendants of the men, women, and children whose tears marked this journey seek to maintain much of their original cultural identity. Many have advocated that the Trail of Tears be designated a historic trail.

illinois
. . . a stuck-up fossil is a state treasure

No, it isn't a loveable furry critter on Sesame Street, nor is it an ogre about to star in the next animated Hollywood block-buster. The Tully Monster is Illinois' official fossil, and it once was a soft-bodied animal that lived in the ocean that covered much of the state 300 million years ago, during the Pennsylvanian Period. The remains of this active, swimming carnivore have been found only in Illinois.

Less than a foot long, the relic had a tail with three fins and a long proboscis that ended in a jaw with eight small, sharp teeth. Talk about snooty . . . the Tully Monster looked down his nose at victims while using it to deliver them as food to the mouth. Drawings show the ancient beast as a fat, flexible sweet potato with roots at each end.

Amateur collector Francis Tully found the first fossil in 1958 and took it to Chicago's Field Museum of Natural History. The specimen defied identification and so became known as the Tully Monster. Paleontologists are still stumped as to what family of animals *Tullinostrum gregarium* belongs. Some think long-lost relatives may be snails and other mollusks.

At least the Tully Monster picked the per-fect spot to be interred and, eventually, remembered. Most of the remnants have been discovered within the Mazon Creek deposits in Will and Grundy Counties, an important repository of fossils in North America. Creatures that died there were rapidly preserved by becoming a hard, per-manent "cast" of ironstone. Think of it as a rocky snapshot for the ages.

Tully Monster:

A snooty ocean creature and the state's official fossil.

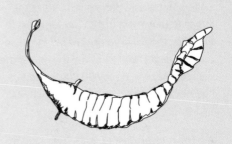

illinois
...the earth moves under your feet

Cast aside every childhood warning you've ever heard about the boogeyman. At Volo Bog State Natural Area, you can hike right into his backyard and come back to tell about it.

Just outside the town of McHenry (45 miles northwest of Chicago), a boardwalk lets you cross what appears to be solid land but is really a quaking quagmire. Layers of floating organic material, mostly sphagnum moss, bubble alongside the boardwalk and rise in eerie lumps called "hummocks." Tamarack trees, a northern species rare to Illinois, use their horizontal root system to help keep the mat together.

It's only natural to dwell on the macabre. After all, the legend of the boogeyman began in a bog—criminals in early England craftily hid from the law in such treacherous places. While bogs can be sinister if you don't watch your step, Volo Bog offers a rare opportunity to explore without getting your feet wet.

When the Wisconsin glacier retreated some 15,000 years ago, small depressions were gouged from the earth where chunks of ice broke free and melted. Most of these basins drained into rivers, but a few that remained landlocked became bogs.

With no drainage, carbon dioxide accumulates and inhibits the bacteria and bugs that promote normal decay. Dead plant life

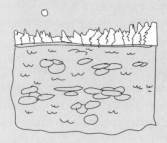

Volo Bog:

A quaking bog that visitors can hike through safely.

piles up, peat forms, and surrounding bog water becomes so acidic that it works like embalming fluid on anything unfortunate enough to fall in.

To enter a bog is to find a world filled with bizarre beauty. Unusual ferns and orchids flourish in the acid environment. So do poison sumac and the carnivorous pitcher plant, which eats insects. More than two dozen threatened or endangered plants can be found at Volo Bog. You'll also see more than 180 different bird species.

Only a handful of bogs exist in Illinois, and they are all located in Lake and McHenry Counties. Volo Bog is the only one that offers safe passage and exhibits all the representative stages in a bog's life, from open water to an oak-hickory forest.

illinois
...one man makes big footprints

Neighbors in the southern Illinois community of Alton always stretched to keep company with their town's loftiest resident. That's because they most likely stood only elbow-high to 8-foot, 11-inch, 490-pound Robert Wadlow, the tallest man ever to walk the face of the earth—with the size 37AAA shoes to prove it.

A lifelong Alton resident, Wadlow weighed a modest 8 pounds, 6 ounces when he was born on February 22, 1918. His parents, Addie and Harold, first suspected trouble when their baby logged 30 pounds at six months. A year later, they were convinced: Toddler Wadlow tipped the scales at 62 pounds.

The culprit was a wacky pituitary gland with a glut of growth hormones. And because 1920s medicine offered no brakes, it was all up, up, and away for Wadlow. He stood 6 feet, 2 inches at age 8 and towered to 8 feet, 4 inches and 390 pounds as an 18-year-old.

Sensitive and smart, the "Gentle Giant" possessed an equally gargantuan heart. He joined the Boy Scouts and the Young Men's Christian Association, collected stamps, loved photography, and even attended college for a year. But simple outings proved to be tall tasks. Seeing a movie required five seats: a seat on either side for his arms, and two in front for his legs. A hotel stay

Wadlow, Robert:

The Alton native who in 1937 became the *Guinness Book of World Records'* tallest man in the world.

meant sleeping crossways atop three double beds.

Wadlow was in good health until age 22, when he developed a fatal infection from one of many blisters that plagued his feet. Emergency surgery and blood transfusions failed, and Wadlow died in his sleep on July 15, 1940. More than 27,000 people attended his funeral. Fearing that their son's body would be examined for medical research, his parents buried him under a concrete slab.

No one has ever filled his shoes, which carried a $100-per-pair price tag in the 1930s, but you can trace his steps via the Wadlow exhibit at the Alton Museum of History and Art (www.altonmuseum.com). Be sure to crane your neck at the nearby Robert Wadlow statue, unveiled in 1985.

illinois
...spit sprouts a town

A stream of saliva may not be the most dignified christening, but no one in the central Illinois town of Lincoln, population roughly 15,000, will argue its potency.

Said spit dates to August 27, 1853, when it was expelled in the form of watermelon juice from the mouth of Abraham Lincoln, then an up-and-coming lawyer. Because the expulsion occurred at a public ceremony recognizing the town named in his honor, some considered the future president's behavior uncouth. Others suggested that he simply may have been ridding himself of some pesky melon seeds.

Regardless, a downtown monument in the shape of a larger-than-life watermelon slice, erected in 1964 by several community organizations, now commemorates the infamous site.

Lincoln boasts that it is "the only city ever named for Abraham Lincoln with his personal consent." Honest Abe served as attorney for the railroad whose construction led to the town's establishment, and he also drew up its incorporation papers. Impressed with their gangly lawyer's abilities, founding fathers asked to borrow his name for their town. Lincoln replied with characteristic humility and humor, noting that "nothing named Lincoln ever amounted to much."

Residents, however, are quick to contest that claim. In addition to the watermelon statue, their town has sprouted Lincoln Christian College and a historical museum brimming with $2.2 million worth of Lincoln-related memorabilia.

For those who argue that the monument should have honored Lincoln, not the watermelon, there's something pretty juicy on the horizon. Seems a movement's underway to erect a $40 million, 305-foot likeness of Abe—as tall as the Statue of Liberty—that would be visible for about 20 miles along Interstate 55.

Now that's something worth spitting about.

Watermelon Statue:

A monument that marks the spot where Abraham Lincoln christened his namesake town with a glob of melon juice.

illinois

... you wait five minutes for the weather to change

Weathered residents of Princeville, Illinois, will forever recall when they made state meteorological history. On January 18–19, 1996, the temperature dropped from 57 degrees to –10 degrees in 24 hours, an amazing 67-degree shift.

Shaking their collective heads, they likely muttered the time-tested truth offered to those less familiar with the state's environmental eccentricities: "If you don't like the weather, wait five minutes."

What you anticipate, however, depends on where you live. Illinois' long, lanky physique—385 miles from north to south—means that Rockford relishes an average annual temperature of 47 degrees, while its southern neighbors in Cairo claim a 59-degree average. Forty-eight inches of rain pelt the south annually, compared to 32 inches in the north.

Illinoisans may use other descriptors, but meteorologists call the climate "continental." Snuggled between warm, moist southern masses and cold, dry air to the north, and far from moderating oceanic influences, Illinois cycles through four seasons of potentially wacky weather. Snow may fall as early as October and as late as May; January brings thunderstorms; June hosts hailstorms. Summer sees soaring temperatures—East St. Louis holds the record at 117 degrees—while winter thermometers plummet, as residents of Con-

gerville, a record-holder at –36 degrees, can attest.

Weather can pack a destructive punch, too. The infamous Tri-State Tornado, the worst in Illinois and United States history, struck on March 18, 1925. Sweeping from southern Missouri to southwestern Indiana, the 1-mile-wide funnel battered Illinois from 2:26 to 4:05 P.M. In a 40-minute period, 541 residents were killed. A snowstorm shut down the Windy City on January 26–27, 1967, dates when Chicago saw a record-breaking 24 inches in 29 hours—a total that stranded 20,000 vehicles and collapsed countless roofs.

Wind, rain, sleet, snow—forecasters do their best to predict any and all. But most folks call it their own way. Morning sunshine? Better grab an umbrella.

Weather:

An atmospheric condition described as "wacky" by Illinoisans and "continental" by meteorologists.

illinois

. . . one man's folly fuels a backyard revolution

Whether billows puff from suburbs or stretch a country mile, there's a smoke signal familiar to every Illinoisan, and it reads "Something's cooking." Could be brats, burgers, chops, or chicken. But chances are better than a bag of charcoal that it's grilling to perfection under a Weber Grill cover.

Legions of backyard chefs, typically male, owe their culinary finesse to a kindred spirit: barbecue buff George Stephen, whose 1951 invention is the world's best-selling charcoal grill.

An employee of Weber Brothers Metal Works who hailed from the Chicago suburb of Palatine, Stephen spent weekdays welding large metal spheres together to make buoys and weekends hunched over his flat, brazier-style grill. Frustrated when wind or rain made his meals a mess, Stephen decided to put a lid on it. Literally.

He fitted a metal grate into one of the spun-metal bowls used for buoy making, fashioned a cover with vents from the same metal, and added three bottom legs and a top handle. Firing up the contraption in his own backyard, Stephen discovered that it not only protected food from the elements, but also transformed the grill into a sort of oven that roasted or barbequed through the heat of glowing coals.

Marketing and production of "George's Kettle"—quickly dubbed "Sputnik" by thou-

Weber Grills:

The world's best-selling kettle-shaped outdoor cooking contraptions, invented and still produced in the Chicago suburb of Palatine.

sands of enthusiastic chefs—began in 1952, and the modest little kettle soon became America's icon for food and fun.

Frivolity continued into the 1960s with the Weber patio grill, and it fired up in the 1970s with gas power and its staple, the Genesis line. Today the inventor's son, Jim Stephen, runs Palatine's Weber Grill plant. Gazing upon the entire operation with seasoned eyes is a bronze statue of its founder.

Tangy backyard flavors also inspired four official Weber restaurants, all in close proximity to Stephen's hometown, that serve barbeque at its best. Got a hankering? Visit www.weber.com for product and restaurant information.

illinois

... white squirrels are privileged residents

Folks in the southeastern town of Olney, known as the Home of the White Squirrels, are nuts about their VIP residents. Laws are written to ensure domestic tranquility for this rare albino breed. A 1925 city ordinance granted white squirrels the right-of-way on town streets; in the case of an unfortunate accident, motorists are slapped with a $25 fine. Take a white squirrel outside the city limits, and you're breaking the law.

Olney's annual census fastidiously tracks its furry population. The official count takes place the last three Saturdays of October, with locals scurrying city streets and documenting every white squirrel seen along their routes. Numbers hold steady at about 200.

Avid squirrel watchers know that the best place to catch sight of the town pets is Olney Park, where the cheeky critters congregate and eschew the low-carb craze by munching on leftover french fries and Oreo cookies. There's even a white squirrel monument here.

Legend has it that white squirrels first scampered into Olney in 1902, when a male and female albino were captured and displayed in a local saloon. Enraged, resident Thomas Tippit Sr. sent his son to the saloon with orders to release the pair in the woods. No sooner had they tasted freedom

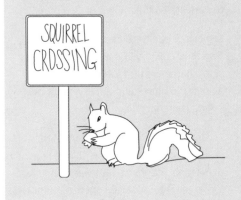

White Squirrels:

A rare breed of bushy-tailed white rodents that pass for residents in Olney.

when a large fox squirrel dropped from a tree, killing the male. Hero Tom Tippit Jr., age 14, shot the would-be attacker as it advanced on the female. Weeks later, white squirrel babies were found in the woods near Tippit's home.

Today the pink-eyed, bushy-tailed town mascot "smiles" from billboards and the uniforms of local policemen and firemen. Residents and tourists go nuts, too—squirreling away key chains, statuettes, postcards, coins, and lapel pins bearing the beloved likeness.

illinois
. . . it's a zoo out there

Howl at the moon. Swim with the swans. Gaze at the giraffes. It's easy to take a walk on the wild side in Illinois. The Chicago area offers two world-class zoological exhibits and the best natural history museum in the nation.

Start at the Lincoln Park Zoo, the oldest in the country. Established in 1868 with the gift of a pair of trumpeter swans, the zoo is now home to more than 1,100 mammals, reptiles, and birds residing on 35 acres of Chicago's lakefront. Its intimate setting enables you to stand toe-to-toe with giraffes and eye-to-eye with lowland gorillas. Two snow-white swans still make their home at the zoo, and swan boat rides are a must-do.

In 1949 Lincoln Park Zoo gained national attention thanks to its director, Marlin Perkins, who hosted a weekly live television series called *Zoo Parade.* He later became famous for the television program *Wild Kingdom.*

Just west of Chicago, Brookfield Zoo has become world renowned for its use of natural barriers, such as moats, rather than cages. It featured the first giant panda exhibit in the United States. One of the most recent additions focuses on wolves and uses one-way viewing windows and cameras to monitor the inside of a den. There's more to a wolf's life than first meets

the eye. Additional viewing areas along a woodland trail allow you to see wolves interact in a natural environment of streams, fallen trees, earth mounds, and wading pools.

You won't find any live animals at the Field Museum, back in Chicago on Lake Shore Drive, but it's brimming with preserved specimens. There you can learn how a species becomes endangered; stroll among Africa's mammals, with everything from aardvarks to zebras; and spend some time with Sue, a full-size *Tyrannosaurus rex.*

For more information, visit www.lpzoo.com, www.brookfieldzoo.org, and www.field museum.org.

The Wild Side:

Where visitors like to walk at two world-class zoos and a renowned natural history museum in the Chicago area.

illinois
. . . someone pops the Peoria question

When politicians or corporations want to take the pulse of America, do they look to the Big Apple, the Windy City, or Los Angeles for answers? Nope. They head to the heart of Illinois and pop the question: "Will it play in Peoria?"

Situated along the Illinois River, halfway between St. Louis and Chicago, this blue-collar town doesn't look or act much different than any other mid-size metropolis. Bingo . . . that's exactly why the cliché has become so universally bantered about. Peoria is the very definition of mainstream, average Americana.

According to local historians, the famous question originated in the 1920s, during Peoria's vaudeville days. When a new live act or stage show was produced, it soon was booked into a Peoria theater. It was believed that if a show could gain the approval of Peoria audiences, it would be successful anywhere in the country. If it didn't receive strong approval in Peoria, the production was often rewritten, recast, or canceled.

The phrase came back into circulation after President Nixon's political advisor, John Ehrlichman, used it when talking about campaigning in the Midwest. Ehrlichman is said to have viewed Peoria as the model of the national norm.

To this day Peoria is used as a national test market for new products and a measure of national trends. To inquire whether something will play in Peoria is quite simply to ask if it will be accepted by America herself.

Will It Play in Peoria?:

A cliché that acts as a barometer of American consumer acceptance.

- POPULAR IN PEORIA
- GOOD
- FAIR
- POOR

illinois
... it's easy to find the Wright stuff

Long before his "retirement," the famous, flamboyant Frank Lloyd Wright had envisioned his legacy: ". . . having a good start, not only do I fully intend to be the greatest architect who has yet lived, but I fully intend to be the greatest architect who will ever live."

Beginning in the 1890s Wright brought bold, radical ideas to the era's popular architectural designs. Dismissing fussy, closed, Victorian "box" homes, he opened wary eyes to structures that melded to the landscape, with rooms that flowed easily into one another. Wright embraced his homes as complete environments, often designing stained glass and furniture to complement the structures. Occasionally, his services included designing gowns in complementary hues for the woman of the house.

Wright perfected his signature "Prairie Style" architecture in Oak Park, a suburb west of Chicago in which he, his wife, and their six children lived from 1889 to 1913. The Wrights' home flaunted what many considered a "wrong" design. Its simple exterior, which combined dark shingles and brick walls with a white stone coping, housed rooms with plentiful windows, fireplaces, and uncovered wood and unpainted plaster walls. Wright also built an adjoining studio where he schooled apprentices.

Wright was restless until the ripe old age of 92, and his output was prolific: He designed

Wright, Frank Lloyd:

Famed architect credited with developing the Prairie Style and designing more than 1,000 structures, a number of which still stand in Oak Park, Illinois.

more than 1,000 structures, about 500 of which were built. His works range from the internationally famous Tokyo Imperial Hotel and New York's Guggenheim Museum to Prairie Style homes in Decatur and Springfield, Illinois. All bear the streamlined shape that he pioneered.

Wright's influence on American architecture is perhaps best modeled in the 25 structures still standing in Oak Park, which claims the world's largest collection of Frank Lloyd Wright designs. Registered as National Historic Landmarks, these homes and buildings annually inspire more than 100,000 visitors, who savor walking tours of the "Wright world."

For more information, contact the Frank Lloyd Wright Preservation Trust at (708) 848–1976.

illinois
... folks have a lot to chew on

In the spring of 1891, little about 29-year-old William Wrigley Jr. foretold his future as founder of a global chewing gum empire. Certainly the names of Wrigley's first brands, Lotta and Vassar, revealed no hints of greatness—and hawking them likely was equally humbling.

Yet this visionary salesman, who arrived in Chicago with $32 in his pocket, never doubted that his products would someday "double the pleasure and double the fun" for millions.

Confidence was rooted in Wrigley's uncanny knack for promotion and one magic word: *premium*. During a brief stint selling baking powder, he gave customers two free packages of chewing gum with each purchase. When gum's popularity dwarfed baking soda's, Wrigley put his money where the mouths were.

In 1893 he introduced Juicy Fruit and Spearmint, both marketed under his name. An advertising pioneer, Wrigley was first in the fledging industry to promote his product via newspapers, magazines, and outdoor posters. He also coined a phrase that still guides the fourth-generation, family-owned business: "Even in a little stick of gum, quality is important."

Nearly as famous as Doublemint, Big Red, and the rest of the packs is company head-quarters—the gleaming white Wrigley Building, two towers connected by a walkway and located along Michigan Avenue, on the Chicago River's north bank. Constructed in 1921, the structure has a unique triangular design patterned after the Seville Cathedral's Giralda Tower in Spain. Nearly 250,000 glazed terra-cotta tiles cover its surface, and a giant two-story clock tells time from multiple directions.

For decades the empire also included ownership of Wrigley Field and a team of celebrated chompers, the Chicago Cubs. Both were sold to the Tribune Company in 1981.

Today Wrigley runs 19 factories worldwide, and big "little sticks" freshen mouths in 180 countries.

Wrigley Company:

The world's largest manufacturer of chewing gum, founded and headquartered in Chicago.

illinois

... the outfield sprouts ivy

If Wrigley Field's ivy-covered walls could talk, they'd tell more tales than ex-Cub Slammin' Sammy Sosa has hit homers.

Constructed in 1914 by restaurant magnate Charlie Weeghman and originally named Weeghman Park, the "friendly confines" are bordered by Clark and Addison Streets in the heart of Chicago. So congenial is the park, in fact, that surrounding blocks are known simply as Wrigleyville.

Chances are, the boys of summers past would still feel right at home here. Rather than trim the ivy that has trailed outfield walls since the 1930s, officials wrote the plant into the rule book: Batters who hit a ball that sticks in the vines earn a ground-rule double. But fans have yet to cheer a slugger who can smack Wrigley's 25-by-75-foot far centerfield scoreboard, a bright-green contraption built in 1937 and still manually operated.

Weeghman eventually was bought out by chewing gum giant William Wrigley Jr., who stepped up to the plate for the park he humbly renamed after himself. His venue was the first to let fans keep home run balls, and when Cubs' followers fretted that vendors blocked their views of the field, Wrigley Field introduced the first perma-nent concession stands. Organ music debuted here, too—a sound that still stirs

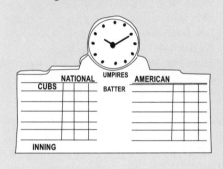

Wrigley Field:

The second oldest ballpark in the major leagues and home to the Chicago Cubs.

the faithful to their feet for the seventh-inning stretch.

With two outs and bases loaded in the bottom of the ninth, Wrigley Field scored as the last ballpark in the country to install lights. Illumination came only after a 1988 ultimatum from the major leagues: Host night games at Wrigley, or head south of the border to archrival St. Louis Cardinals turf for postseason play.

101

index

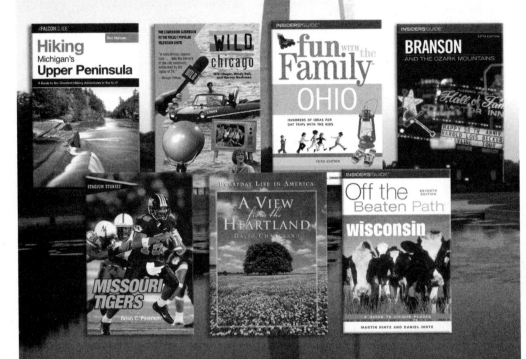